PERSUA

WRITING FOR

BUSINESS

PERSUASIVE WRITING FOR BUSINESS

How to write proposals, letters, emails
and other business communications to
influence, impress and persuade.

> *"Patrick has a lucid and elegant style of writing which allows
> him to present information in a way that is organised, focused
> and easy to apply"* (Professional Marketing Magazine).

PATRICK FORSYTH

bookshaker

First Published in Great Britain in 2014
by www.BookShaker.com

© Copyright Patrick Forsyth

ABOUT THE BOOK

HOW TO WRITE EFFECTIVE LETTERS, emails, proposals – in fact any document that must present a case and do so persuasively.

In this straightforward and practical book Patrick Forsyth sets out clear guidelines on how to define your message clearly and present it in writing in a powerful and persuasive way that is likely to prompt agreement and action more certainly. The advice here is tried and tested and designed to help you achieve results and make an outstanding impression on clients/customers and others to whom you need to write.

Patrick Forsyth is a consultant, trainer and writer and the author of more than 100 books for those working as executives and managers in organisations of all sorts.

AUTHOR'S NOTE

I HAVE WRITTEN MANY BUSINESS books (see information at the end of this text) and many of them are available for download from their respective publishers or on line booksellers; this one is available in print and for download.

The book is specifically designed with both formats in mind; however you read it, it is designed to provide a succinct guide, one focusing on the key approaches and presenting practical tips and guidelines that will enable the reader to go away and do things differently and, perhaps, better.

If you read this and want to get in touch, then my web site is www.patrickforsyth.com and will allow you to email me.

Patrick Forsyth
Touchstone Training & Consultancy
28 Saltcote Maltings
Maldon
Essex CM9 4QP
United Kingdom

CONTENTS

INTRODUCTION

*"I write when I'm inspired, and I see to it
that I'm inspired at nine o'clock every morning"*

Peter De Vries

COMMUNICATIONS IS AN INHERENT PART of business.
Yet successful communication can be difficult. Poor
communication can cause problems. This may involve a
momentary hiatus as two people try to sort out exactly
what is meant. Or it may cause a major misunderstanding
that causes a project of some sort to be stopped in its
tracks. Why is this? There are many reasons, but one
is certainly an assumption that what is being done is
not difficult, coupled with a subsequent unwillingness
to check out the principles on which success might be
based. Perhaps that is actually two reasons already, and
more are investigated in the first chapter.

Furthermore some kinds of communication are
inherently more difficult than others. The intentions
of communication may vary. It may need to inform,
explain, motivate, challenge, prompt a debate or more;
and such intentions are not mutually exclusive, one
communication may need to do several of these things
at once. Communications designed to be persuasive adds
another layer and putting something in writing can add
further complications. I once stayed in a hotel with a
sign inside the bedroom door saying: *In the interests of*

security please ensure your bedroom door is firmly shut before entering or leaving the room. It would be a good trick if you can do it, and that is just one sentence. Someone wrote it, printed it and posted it around the hotel and still no one noticed it was rubbish!

You want me to do *what*?

So, any communicating clearly needs some care. Even when care is being taken additional complications may contrive to compound the problems. Certain intentions are harder to achieve than others, and high on this list must be that of *persuasion*. For sake of example, let us assume that you are reading this in a bookshop as you decide whether or not to buy the book. I want you to buy it; the royalties may be small, but they do mount up! If I just put to you the thought - *Buy it!* - then your response might well be simply to say *"No"*. After all, why should you? You might not care if my income remains nil for the next ten years. However, if I tell you that the book will help you get your own way more often and more certainly. If I say that it will enable you to put over a more powerful persuasive case in future, and that it is quick and straightforward to take on board the lessons spelt out here - then you might consider the matter more carefully. If these last statements coincide with your actually needing to put over an important, persuasive case in the near future then maybe, just maybe, you will buy the book. Go on, you have read more than enough now if you are standing in a bookshop - have you no shame? – go to the cash point now. Sorry, I digress. The point is that just telling someone to do something is not guaranteed to persuade them actually to *do* something. You have to build a case, put it over clearly and ... but we are getting ahead of ourselves: the point is that it needs the proper approach.

On paper

There is a further problem, and that is that most people are better at communicating face to face than in other ways. Other methods all do have their disadvantages. The telephone is good, immediate, maybe quick and easy, but try describing to someone over the telephone how to, say, tie a shoelace. Think about it for a second. You know how to do it, you could easily show someone else - but, on the telephone, using only your voice, it is somehow more of a problem.

One method that seems consistently to render people less articulate is when they have to put something in writing. Your manager wants a note about it, the Board need a report or proposal, and my editor wants a book (and there are still twenty something thousand words to go). Business writing almost seems to hinder good communication. People who can talk about something and usually get their message over successfully, find themselves descending into a muddle of business-speak and gobbledegook, writing something over formal, over long and - at worst - forgetting somewhere along the way exactly what their objectives were in the first place.

Of course, putting something into written form can be a pain, and its being so can extend the task as agonising over the best form of words to make permanent takes time. Hence this book: the intention here is clear. It is to assist the process of communicating successfully and persuasively when it must be done in writing. This may mean a letter (or often an e-mail), or it may mean a report or, more likely, a proposal and various kinds of letter and document in between. It might also mean copy for a brochure or a newsletter. A message may be sent internally: to a group of staff or an individual member of your team - or upwards, perhaps to your manager. It may be sent externally: to a supplier, a customer or to many customers (this latter may include direct mail letters). The circumstances can vary. But the intention is always the same. It is to put over a case to someone else that will succeed in persuading them to your point to view, and often to prompt them to take action as a result.

Whatever your circumstances, this book is designed to help you see more clearly how to go about writing persuasively. In turn it describes the nature of what acts to persuade, as understanding this can be used to help you present a message, which will be seen as persuasive. There is no one magic formula, as so often what makes a business technique work is, though it may be based on certain fundamental approaches, a matter of attention to a number of details. Certainly that is the case here.

It is, however, possible. You *can* write a clear, persuasive case if you go about it in the right way and, if you do that, you will also begin to do it faster as well. In a busy life that is something worthwhile too. In the next few chapters we will see how all this can be done, starting with a look at some of the difficulties of communication and how to avoid them.

Patrick Forsyth
Touchstone Training & Consultancy,
28 Saltcote Maltings, Maldon,
Essex CM9 – 4QP, United Kingdom

What you will learn

This guide will make sure that you:

- Understand the role of the written word in communication and business relationships
- Know what people expect of written communications and how it possible to impress as well as inform
- Set clear objectives for your messages
- Get appropriate words down easily and quickly and minimise editing
- Structure messages for best effect
- Adopt the right style to project corporate and personal personality and strike a distinctive note
- Make your message truly persuasive
- Use language to augment your message and enhance its power
- Fit your message to the method you use (letter, email etc.)
- Get the response, and agreement, that you want.

1. PERSUASION:
THE FIRST PRINCIPLES

IN THIS CHAPTER WE LOOK at how to achieve understanding, at anticipating difficulties and utilising human nature to create a secure foundation for our communication and persuasion.

As we have seen, being persuasive is a form of communication, albeit a form of some complexity. As such it is unlikely to succeed unless it utilises the basic principles of successful communication. If you use every endeavour to ensure your communication is clear then this will act as a firm foundation for your intention to persuade. Persuasion must build a case for its proposition. You cannot persuade people to do just anything. For example, if I asked you to send me a cheque for a six-figure sum I might well find that no argument could successfully gain your compliance (though if you are the exception, do let me know!). But given something where you deem persuasion could be made to work, it is surely no more than common sense that people will never be persuaded if they do not really understand the case you are promoting.

The secret power of clarity
Beyond the obvious premise of being understood, a second advantage of clarity is that it can be, of itself, impressive. If your argument is complex, and if you

marshal the facts and put them over in a clear, logical and understandable way, then people read a competence into what you do. Your stance itself adds credibility, it suggests that what you say is not only understandable, but worth listening to and maybe worth acting on. Your ability to explain and make things clear does not guarantee that you will succeed in persuading, but it is a good start. To reinforce this point, think of the opposite. What does a muddled, ill-thought out case say to you? Likely it says that whoever is making it is struggling because it just is not an easy case to make.

How people receive communications

Two or more people are involved when you communicate, and it makes sense to be aware of the situation of *both* parties. Its originator may bungle a communication, but the people on the receiving end can also act to make things difficult. They do not even have to try; human nature is such that people act inherently in a way that makes it necessary for those communicating to work harder. The main ways this happens are as follows:

- **Inattention**: people just do not concentrate. They focus on what seems to *them* to be important, and may make wrong assumptions based on half the message. They read something and say to themselves *I know where this is going*. Then they skim the next bit and end up missing an important element of the message.

So: you must work at getting peoples' attention. In writing, this means making sure you *earn a reading*, and that your writing is interesting, that it flows and also that it *looks* readable (which is why a book like this has lots of headings and a layout that breaks it up into bite sized pieces).

- **Incomprehension:** misunderstanding occurs in a number of ways. Particularly this is the case through unwarranted comparison (people say *this seems like so and so*, and make assumptions based on past circumstances rather than what is actually in front of them). Also ill-judged use of jargon (this, which includes technical terms, abbreviations etc. can be a useful shorthand between people in the know, but can easily confuse when the level is wrongly pitched). For example, when I sent this book to the publisher I referred to it as a m/s – a manuscript – a term that was appropriate between the two of us, but which might not be more widely understood. This effect is compounded by any neglect in painting a clear picture, when more than just the bare details are necessary.

  So expect achieving understanding to need working at, make sure writing is suitably descriptive and people are not blinded by inappropriately stated technicalities.

- **Suspicion:** people have a natural suspicion of those "with something to sell", and assume that, whatever you want, it is likely to be better for you than for them.

So: if you are to allay their suspicions, your writing needs to make a strong case, one that relates as much to other peoples' point of view as your own.

- **Inaction:** often people are unwilling to act because doing so goes against a habit or is seen as exposing them to risk: *If I do this and it doesn't work out, what then?*

- *So* your writing must actively *prompt* action, not assume that the case itself will do so.

- **Hidden feelings:** the response you get to a written message may not be all it seems. People may hide or misrepresent their feelings and necessary feedback cannot then be taken at face value. For example, someone may rule something out not because the case for it is flawed, but because they do not fully understand it and do not want to appear stupid by saying so.

- *So:* feedback needs to be teased out and, even then, it needs to be interpreted by checking or "reading between the lines".

Not only will your attempts to persuade be more likely to succeed if you bear such inherent difficulties in mind, but you can ease their effect by taking advantage of other aspects of human nature that help.

Responding to inherent difficulties

Achieving understanding is more likely, however, if certain things are born in mind; they can then act like oil on an awkward cog-wheel to make things go more smoothly. The key principles here include:

- **Focussing on other's viewpoint:** peoples' first response to most messages is a question – *what does it mean for me?* They look for either positive or negative effects, but are apt to see any negative ones first. It is sensible therefore to accept that this will happen and accommodate it. Writing simply that - *costs must be reduced* – may instigate worries of various sorts about someone's job, while writing that – *to secure our ability to maintain the full team and deliver the standard of service that customers' want, we must seek ways of reducing costs* can change the initial response. There may still be questions, but it can be seen that people's fears are being addressed (and the detail may spell out more).

- **Utilising other's experience:** every message is considered alongside someone's past experience. Write about a project and they think of another – *just like it* – and if they are not, in fact, similar this can cause difficulties. So the rules here are to know something of other's experience (or check it out), to make specific links and to avoid unwarranted assumptions being made. It may help to make comparisons, either writing that *this is very like the X project you will remember* ...or saying *this is not exactly like* ... and explaining in either case to make a clear distinction.

- **Making it logical:** the structure of a message is important. If the structure is unclear, or not there, then any case will be more difficult to follow. It is *not* a question of what is easiest to write, rather what will make best sense to other people. Choose a logical sequence and arrangement for what you write and that alone will play a part in ensuring its acceptance. Also important here is to start with an overview and then go into detail, rather than just launching into a lengthy explanation of whatever comes first. The three rules here are to make sure there is a logic: that it makes sense not just to you but to your reader(s), and that you tell them what it is (and, if necessary, why you have adopted this particular way forward).

- **Repeating your message:** repetition is basic to human understanding. This does *not* mean key sentences need to be repeated verbatim, but it may well mean that things should be repeated in different ways. Sometimes this goes beyond one communication: a note is circulated spelling out a topic for discussion at a meeting, the meeting goes through it again and matters are summarised in a note after the meeting. Sometimes it means tackling something in different ways, as for example figures can be given weight by being presented as figures and in a graph. Using appropriate forms of repetition to reinforce understanding and enhancing the persuasiveness of your case is a simple, yet useful technique. Using appropriate forms of repetition ... sorry, point made.

There is an old saying that *it is difficult to see the writing on the wall when your back's to it*. Similarly the message here is straightforward: it can be difficult for people to read, and be persuaded by, your messages when the way they have been written either ignores:

- The ways in which readers will find receiving the message difficult
- Methods that could have been used to make that reception easier.

A good persuasive message, that is one with a real chance of success, will not just set out what you want in your terms and, as it were, in isolation. Rather it will address its reader(s) and will work *with* them to put things over in terms that they will understand and relate to - and with which, therefore, they may ultimately agree. Sometimes recognising just one key factor can make the difference, see box.

Looking forward not back

In a new job and charged with making radical changes, Mary found every plan she put forward to her boss was rejected. An examination of the tone of her proposals showed why. She was writing something that said something like – *This system is not working well and could be corrected by* ...albeit coupled with a perfectly sensible suggestion. But who had originated the system she planned

---

to change? Her boss. In effect she was saying: *Your system's no good, I can suggest something better.* A change of tone to one that positioned the change carefully in time terms – *This system has worked well in the past; in future we must find a way of also accommodating ...so building in the following changes will ...* reversed the reaction. It really was only the implied criticism of past action that produced the negative reaction. A minor change to the way such proposals were written was enough to change the outcome. Such seemingly minor matters are often instrumental in dictating outcomes.

The foundation is important – you will not persuade anyone about anything that they do not clearly understand. That said there is more to understand and use regarding what actually acts to make people decide to agree with something. Chapter 2 looks at how people make decisions and how therefore we can assist them to make the ones we want.

Summary
The first prerequisite of making a persuasive case is to:

- Understand and recognise why communication can be difficult for both "sender and receiver"
- Act to get round this and create a solid foundation of understanding on which a persuasive case can be built.

2. Assembling a Persuasive Case

IN THIS CHAPTER WE EXAMINE how you should view the process of being persuasive and how, by recognising what others are doing in the same circumstances, we can work *with* people to create mutual agreement

Now, recognising the difficulties of making communication work, we go beyond them and look at what creates a message that acts to persuade, and see how your writing can relate to the way in which people make decisions to act.

People are often suspicious of someone "with something to sell". Persuasion is synominous with selling and selling does not have a very good image. Consider your own reaction to someone trying to sell you double glazing or insurance, particularly when it is done inexpertly or inappropriately; every persuasive message prompts a little of the reaction generated by the worst kind of selling.

The process in view

Your approach must reduce and get over this kind of feeling. How do you do this? Essentially you start by adopting the right attitude to the process. Before you write anything you are going to need to approach it in the right way. Persuading someone must *not* be regarded as a process of "doing something to people". Rather it should be seen as working *with* people. After all any communication inherently involves more than one person. People presented with a possible course of action will want to make up their own minds about it; indeed they will instinctively weigh up the case presented to them and make a considered decision.

The amount of conscious weighing up undertaken will depend on the import of the decision to be made. Ask someone in the office - *will you spare time for a drink at lunchtime so that we can discuss the next scheduled departmental meeting?* - and they may hardly need to think about it at all. It is only a few minutes, they have to have a bite to eat anyway, and they already know about the meeting and want to be involved. Ask, or write to them, about something more substantial and the weighing up process will involve more; maybe much more.

If you want to define persuasion it is perhaps best described as being a process of helping people weigh something up and make a decision about it. Literally when you aim to persuade, you are *helping people decide*. It follows therefore that you need to understand how they actually go about this process. In simple terms, paraphrasing psychologists who have studied it, this thinking process can be described thus, people:

- Consider the factors that make up a case
- Seek to categorise these as advantages or disadvantages
- Weigh up the complete case, allowing all the pluses and minuses

- Select a course of action (which may be simply agreeing or not, or involve the choice of one action being taken rather than another), which reflects the overall picture.

Let us be clear. What is going on here is not a search for perfection. Most things we look at have some downsides; this may be the most useful book you ever read, but reading it does take a little time, and that could be used for something else. This time disappearing might well be seen as a downside. The weighing scales analogy is worth keeping in mind. It can act as a practical tool, helping you envisage what is going on during what is intended to be a persuasive exchange. Beyond that it helps structure the process if you also have a clear idea of the sequence of thinking involved in this weighing up process.

The thinking process

One way of look at what is going on, is to think of people moving through several stages of thinking, as it were saying to themselves:

- **I matter most.** Whatever you want me to do, I expect you to worry about how I feel about it, respect me and consider my needs
- **What are the merits and implications of the case you make?** Tell me what you suggest and why it makes sense (the pluses) and whether it has any snags (the minuses) so that I can weigh it up; bearing in mind that few, if any, propositions are perfect

- **How will it work?** Here people additionally want to assess the details not so much about the proposition itself but about the areas associated with it. For example, you might want to persuade someone to take on, or become involved with, a project. The idea of the project might appeal, but say it ends with them having to prepare a lengthy written report, they might see that as a chore and therefore as a minus and might, if the case is finely balanced, reject it because of that
- **What do I do?** In other words what action - exactly - is now necessary? This too forms part of the balance. If something seen in a quick flick through this book persuaded you that it might help you, you may have bought it. In doing so you recognised (and accepted) that you would have to read it and that this would take a little time. The action – reading – is inherent in the proposition and, if you were not prepared to take it on, this might have changed your decision.

It is after this thinking is complete that people will feel they have sufficient evidence on which to make a decision. They have the balance in mind, and they can compare it with that of any other options (and remember, some choices are close run with one option only just coming out ahead of others). Then people can decide; and feel they have made a sensible decision, and done so on a considered basis.

This thinking process is largely universal. It may happen very quickly and might be almost instantaneous – the snap judgement. Or it may take longer, and that may sometimes indicate days or weeks (or longer!) rather than minutes or hours. But it is always in evidence. Because of this, there is always merit in setting out your case in a way that sits comfortably alongside the way in which it will be considered. Hence: the definition that describes persuasion as *helping the decision making process.*

This thinking process should not be difficult to identify with; it is what you do too. Essentially all that is necessary when attempting to persuade is to keep it in mind and address the individual questions in turn. Thus you need to:

- **Start by demonstrating a focus on the other person** – it helps also to aim to create some rapport and make clear how you aim to put things over (making clear, for example, how you plan to go through something)
- **Present a balanced case** – you need to stress the positive, of course, but not to pretend there are no snags, especially if manifestly there are some, so present a clear case, give it sufficient explanation and weight and recognise the balancing up that the recipient will undertake
- **Add in working details** – mention how things will work, include ancillary details especially those that will matter to others.

In this way, when you set out a case the structure and logic of it should sensibly follow this pattern. Otherwise the danger is that you will be trying to do one thing while the person you are communicating with is doing something else. They will do what they want, and especially so when they are reading something - and you are not there to try to draw them back to your logic.

Persuasion's magic formula

There is, if not quite a magic formula, certainly one core principle that can help make every message you write more persuasive. This is the concept of what are called *benefits*. People do not buy products and services, and the same goes for ideas or anything else, they buy what these things *do for or mean to them*. I do not want a laptop computer for its own sake, but I do want to be able to write quickly and easily on the move. *Features* of the machine, that is its: size, weight, portability, battery life etc. are not ends in themselves, they are only interesting or relevant because of how they produce benefits. Thus the low weight makes the machine portable, which means that I can stick it in my brief case and write on an aeroplane journey and the increased productivity (or perhaps greater earnings) is the ultimate benefit.

The relationship here is important. Benefits are made possible or produced by features and if they are relevant to someone then telling them about them is the best core content for a persuasive message. Benefits may be:

- Tangible or intangible (in the computer example the status of being seen to have the latest and lightest machine, may be as important to some people as the more tangible benefit of several hours work being done while travelling abroad)

- Personal (it is valuable to *me* to be able to work on the move)
- Corporate (it is profitable to *my company* for me to be able to work on the move)
- Important to *other people someone is concerned about* (perhaps I am buying laptops for me and other members of staff and their feelings are important too)

Benefits must always be relevant. Strictly the fact that a car has a five-speed gearbox, which will be more economic (feature) and cost less to run (benefit), is only an advantage if running costs actually matter. Someone buying an expensive sports car may be in a position not to care.

The task here therefore is first to look at the case you plan to make, and to analyse it in terms of its features and benefits. If you list things (benefits on the left as they should most often be stated first, features on the right) then you will see how they interlock. One feature can produce several benefits (as the car's five speed gearbox is instrumental in producing a number of things: better fuel economy, less wear and tear on the engine at high speeds and less noise too). Then you can think about how you describe them. If a benefit is written of in descriptive terms then it becomes that much stronger in how it can positively affect your case.

Benefits in action

Thus: you could say something will *save you money* (saving something you want to save is always a benefit, as is gaining anything positive), or that it will *save money and recoup its cost in a month,* or *it will half what you spend.* If the description matches the circumstances of the reader and if it specifically rings bells because of how it is described then this will work best. Consider a product example. A company sells cookery equipment to restaurants and cafes. One product is a flat grill. One feature is its size, there are various models and one has a cooking surface of 800 square centimetres. What is the benefit? *It will cook a dozen eggs or six steaks simultaneously.* Now most people find it difficult to conjure up 800 square centimetres in their minds eye, but *everyone* who runs a restaurant will be able to imagine the eggs and steaks with no problem at all. Link the way this is described to their situation further – *imagine the rush you get at breakfast time* – and it makes a powerful point.

If you always keep in mind what something does for or means to other people you will be able to write text that will put over a more powerful case. The phrase "benefit-led" is used in selling and that is a good way of thinking about it. Benefits come first, features explain how that is possible and, if necessary, you can add additional credibility (that is evidence or proof – something other than you saying *it's good.*

For example: *This book is called "Persuasive Writing for Business"* (feature). *It will help you make a persuasive case and obtain agreement from others* (benefit), *which will save arguments and get more done* (further benefit). *Its methods are tried and tested and their presentation in training courses has received positive feedback* (evidence, to which might be added a positive comment from a named delegate or training organisation). The idea of teasing out the way you put things by saying *which means that* ... and seeing where that takes you is a good one; start with a feature and at the end of the line you will assuredly have a benefit, maybe more than one.

Incidentally, proof – some evidence that is objective (i.e. not just you saying that it is good) – is an important component of the argument. Never just rely on your own say so, but seek and build in evidence. This could be sheer numbers (*thousands of customers can't be wrong*), or tests, guarantees or standards met or complied with. We touched earlier on a car as an example. If the distributor says the car will do *50 miles per gallon*, do you believe them, or assume that some exaggeration may be involved? How about if they say *independent tests in this motoring magazine show it does 50 mph?* No contest.

You can do worse than list all the things that people might obtain from your offering prior to writing. Some may be classic, see box, others may be more individual to whatever you are writing about.

> **What's in it for me?**
>
> As a result of agreeing with you, people might be able to:
>
> - Make more money
> - Save money
> - Save time, effort or hassle
> - Be more secure
> - Sort out problems
> - Be able to exploit opportunities
> - Motivate others (e.g. staff)
> - Impress people (e.g. customers)

Your chosen manner

Now with the core aspects that make your case in mind, you need to think more about how to put it over. The way your message is approached is also important. For example, if, as soon as even a few lines are read, it is clear that you are taking it for granted that agreement will follow, and if this seems inappropriately arrogant then the likelihood is that it will not be taken so seriously.

The approach taken to putting over your case should be:

- **Well considered:** if it has clearly been banged down in haste and without thought the case will be given less credence
- **Well projected:** it should have the courage of its convictions, everything about the way it is

expressed – language, style and argument - should add to its power (we return to such factors later)

- **Empathetic:** in other words it should come over as respecting other peoples' points of view and seeing things from their perspective.

Empathy is perhaps especially important. If it is well in evidence it prevents other elements – however persuasively put – coming over as unreasonable or "pushy". A balanced approach is necessary here. If everything is piled on to create more and more persuasive power, then the message becomes strident and what is being done becomes self-defeating. If persuasion is tempered with empathy then the whole becomes more acceptable.

If a written message follows these principles then already it has a better chance of succeeding. So far so good. But there is more. In the next chapter we look at defining the totality of what needs to be done and thus deciding how to go about expressing it.

Summary

For the moment remember that:

- It helps to think of persuasion as helping people to decide
- Your logic must therefore reflect theirs
- The essence of being persuasive is to make it easy for people to make a decision, and do so in a way that makes your suggested action seem the best choice.

3. A FOUNDATION FOR SUCCESS

IN THIS CHAPTER FOUR ELEMENTS that contribute to the ultimate success of the message are considered: defining your message, deciding how to present it, reflecting the reader's expectations and projecting the right personal profile.

Writing something down may seem like the part of the task here that is complicated, but it is made significantly easier by action - thinking - that is undertaken ahead of writing anything at all. You will also find it quicker to write things when you have done some appropriate thinking beforehand. The time equation here is significant. If a part of the total time is spent in preparation, this does not just shorten the writing time (and reduce any editing needed); it actually shortens the whole task. So, no apologies, but I will hold off discussing actually writing something for a little longer.

Setting clear objectives

The first stage here is easily stated. You must ask yourself why - *why exactly* - you are communicating. The power of this is in the detail and in creating clear objectives; this is not an academic point, objectives are not just "good things" to have - they give what you do direction. Consider a simple example. You have to persuade a group of people to reduce costs in their department. Right, but what exactly does this mean? Does even saving the price of a box of paperclips mean they will have done what you want? Probably not. "Reducing costs" is not a clear objective. It is not specific, it cannot be measured, and it specifies no timing. As such it hardly helps as a basis for deciding what to write. Stating the objective as to "reduce departmental administrative costs by 15% in the next six months" is clear. Stated thus, it will make it easier to write something designed to get people to do exactly that (and, not least, that will enable them to *know* exactly what they are expected to do). If the figure is realistic (if it can be done without jeopardising operational quality), and achievable (it is actually possible to make such a reduction) then the case to do so may well be accepted, and action will successfully be prompted.

Underrating the need to set clear objectives is dangerous; a document that is just "about" something never has the same authority or credibility and is never as likely to persuade.

Three key questions

Once you have set clear objectives can you start drafting something? Not yet, also before you write there are three further questions the answers to which you should be clear about. They are:

1. **What are your intentions?**

The main one is clear: you want to *persuade* someone to agree with your point of view or to take action - or both. There may be other things you need to do as well. For example:

- *Motivate*: creating personal enthusiasm and feeling for something that will make persuasion easier to achieve
- *Prompt debate*: the first step to agreement might be a discussion, perhaps what you write needs to make that seem desirable
- *Link back to past communications*: this is often the case and, of course, the form of past communications may vary from a meeting to an earlier letter
- *Instruct or demonstrate*: this may be an important preliminary to understanding.

Finally – and always – you need to *inform*: passing a clear message and description to someone, and bearing in mind that people rarely agree to anything when they do not understand.

Thinking about this and having your intentions clear in your mind is an important step, and will make it easier to write something in due course. It is especially useful if there is any sort of complexity – you may well be trying to achieve a number of things – and this will help you to get things straight in your mind.

2. **What do your readers expect?**
The answer here only really needs a little empathy. Imagine yourself in the mind of your reader. What would

you want? As well as being *understandable,* probably something:

- *Readable:* that is that flows, the language of which is simple and there is guidance from the structure, headings etc. to help them through
- *Manageable:* I choose this word particularly. Many readers might specify brief, but they want to know enough about things, so it describes it better to say that a case must be put succinctly. This should still allow it to be sufficiently short to look manageable
- *At the right level:* in terms of any technical content and in terms of complexity
- *Interesting:* well, so far as is possible, certainly with business communication sometimes this will be a real challenge; however, many unlikely things - say a note asking (persuading) people to take voluntary redundancy – can be given interest with some thought.

3. **What profile are you trying to project?**

This will depend on what you do, who you are and to whom you are writing. Consider: would the case you make be more likely to be accepted from one kind of person rather than another? It is natural for judgements to be made, in part, on the basis of an individual's credibility (thus you probably take more notice of your accountant on financial matters than of your bookmaker).

A wealth of characteristics may be involved here, but consider just one initially. You may benefit from appearing well-organised. However well organised you may be this is a characteristic that can be projected, and if necessary exaggerated. And the same is true of all such factors, if you want to appear expert, experienced, approachable, prepared, caring, sincere; or as if you have done your research, explored various possibilities, minimised the difficulties or whatever. All these can be projected: all you need to do is consider what characteristics you need to stress and then work at putting them over. Some may shine through effortlessly; others may need a degree of contrivance, or exaggeration.

Again this is an important factor. I hope that, if you have read this far, then you may now believe that I know something about business writing and about persuasive writing in particular. If so there is only one way this can have come about – because my writing gives that impression. After all, unless we have met, you probably know very little about me. Projection needs to be an inherent part of your writing.

Ready to write

If you have a clear idea in mind of exactly what the task facing you consists of, then the actual task of getting something down in writing will be easier. Such a view needs to be broad. If you write having only half thought it through, then the danger is that your writing may not incorporate everything you want. The job of editing something is then made very much more difficult as you go back and try to add in an element originally omitted.

There is always a danger that, rather than your writing flowing, it will give the impression of having been produced in disparate bits; as too may the argument it presents.

Now, finally, with all this in mind you are ready to write something. If you adopt a systematic way of composing and editing what you write will also help make your chosen words appropriate for the job in hand, so it is to such an approach that we turn next.

Summary

Before you write *anything* you need to:

- Set clear objectives (so that you are clear *why* you are writing)
- Decide and prioritise your intentions (to make sure you achieve *everything* necessary)
- Decide how you must come across and how this will help make the message persuasive
- Bear the likes, dislikes, motivations and expectations of the chosen recipient(s) of your message in mind so that the message is written for them, rather than just in the way it strikes you.

A case of good intentions

Having summarised the content of this chapter we will pause and take stock. If you are going to compose persuasive text, then it is useful to have an example in mind of what to avoid. Consider as an example a simple, but important, sales letter; the kind of thing sent in response to a customer enquiry. The letter reproduced here was sent to me after I had telephoned asking about possible accommodation for a training seminar at a hotel. Read it through.

Dear Mr Forsyth

Following my telephone call with you of yesterday I was delighted to hear of your interest in the XYZ Hotel for a proposed meeting and luncheon some time in the future.

I have pleasure in enclosing for your perusal our banqueting brochure together with the room plan and, as you can see, some of our rooms could prove most ideal for your requirement.

At this stage, I would be more than happy to offer you our delegate rate of (*) to include the following:

* morning coffee with biscuits
* 3-course luncheon with coffee
* afternoon tea and biscuits
* flip chart, pads and pencils
* room hire and visual aid equipment
* Service and tax
and I trust this meets with your approval.

> Should you at any time wish to visit our facilities and discuss your particular requirements further, please do not hesitate to contact me but, in the meantime, if you have any queries on the above, I would be very pleased to answer them.
>
> Yours sincerely

* *Note:* the proposed charge per person per day was included here.

Just consider this letter for a moment.

While no doubt well intentioned and polite and containing a certain amount of information, it does not really begin to *sell* in an appropriate manner. Nor does it project a useful image. In this respect it is sadly not so untypical in style; many such letters are similarly bland.

Let us look at it again (from the beginning):

- It links to my enquiry but has a weak, formula, start (and no heading). I do not want to know about their delight (of course they want my business), starting with something about me would be better
- I am not running a "meeting and luncheon", I explained it was a training session - this is their terminology not mine
- The event is not "at some time in the future"; I quoted a date (this and the points above tell us it is in all likelihood a standard letter)

- Next we have more of their pleasure. I am more interested in what the brochure will do for me, rather than what their sending it does for them. And, yes, people really do use words like "perusal" in writing, though it seems very old fashioned to most people - and who would *say* it?
- "Banqueting brochure" is jargon, their terminology again (though it may well be useful and I do like to get a room plan)
- Do they have a suitable room or not? The words "some of our rooms could ...." are simply unclear
- The section about costs starts with the words "At this stage". But I am sure they do not mean to say "we will negotiate later". The phrase is padding, and akin to people who start every sentence with the word "basically"
- Most will find the list okay, but is it right to ask if it "meets with our approval"?
- People who use hotels nearly always want to see something like a meeting room in advance, so the text would be better to assume that and make arranging it straightforward. Also the writer might better have maintained the initiative and said they would get in touch (they never did, incidentally)
- Suggesting there may be queries is again wrong. Why? It is the wrong word - are they suggesting the letter is inadequate, or that something is bound not to be understandable? Talking about "additional information" would be wholly different; and better

- The cumulative effect of their delight and pleasure - five references - is somewhat over the top. They are doing everything but touching their forelock, especially if there are additional things that might be more usefully said instead.

You may find other matters to comment on also. The punctuation is scarce, for example. Certainly the net effect does not stand up to any sort of analysis bearing in mind its intention is to impress a potential customer. It easily falls into the "bad example" category.

Exercise

So, how might it be better done? If you want to undertake a little exercise then you might pause here and have a go at rewriting it in a better manner. Alternatively undertake a similar analysis on something of your own, or from within your own organisation, and rewrite that. Otherwise we will leave it here for the moment, but will return to it and examine an *alternative* version - there is, of course, no such thing as one "correct" version – later, having continued our review of how to compose persuasive words.

It may be useful to bear the ways in which this goes wrong in mind as we move on. Next, we look at getting something down on paper.

4. WRITE ON: GETTING THE WORDS DOWN

IN THIS SHORT CHAPTER YOU will be given a simple formula for systematic writing. It is a proven format (writing this book was approached in exactly this way), one that can:

- Make the writing process faster to execute
- Make initial text require less amendment
- Ensure that the finished version of the text is more likely to be right for the job it is intended to do.

First, remember the preparation advocated in the last chapter. You should now be clear about your purpose in writing, about your specific objectives and you should have your potential or actual reader(s) and their point of view in mind. Now you can concentrate on *what* you have to say (and not say, for that matter) and *how* you are going to put it.

A systematic approach
The following provides a pathway. You can follow it or adapt it. You can shortcut it somewhat especially for straightforward bits of work, but not too much – omitting significant elements of the different stages can make writing slower, more awkward and allow the end result to be less good than would otherwise be the case.

Stage 1: research

This may or may not be necessary. It may be that everything you need to have to hand is in your head. On the other hand it may be that you need to do some digging, or at the least some assembling. For example, let us suppose you are writing about one of your company's products. It may make sense to get together previous documents describing it, technical literature, even the product itself, and have these to hand as you commence the job. It may be that you need to cast the net wider; in this case what about examining competitive product material, for example?

There is no hard and fast rule here. You should, however ask yourself what might be useful and take a moment to collect and look at or read what the task suggests is necessary.

Stage 2: list the content

Next, forgetting about sequence, structure and arrangement, just list – in short note (or keyword) form – every significant point you might want to make. Give yourself plenty of space; certainly use one sheet of paper as it lets you see everything at a glance without turning over. Put the points down, as they occur to you, at random across the page. *Note:* some – many – of these will need to be stated in benefit form (as discussed in Chapter 2).

You will find that this process (which is akin to mindmapping) acts as a good thought prompter. It enables you to fill out the picture as one thing leads to another, with the freestyle approach removing the need to think or worry about anything else or even linking points together. The scale of this stage may vary. Sometimes it is six words on the back of an envelope, more often somewhat more on an A4 sheet (and this book started life on a sheet of flipchart paper divided into squares for the chapters).

Stage 3: sorting it out

Now you can bring some sort of order to bear. Review what you have noted down and decide:

- On the sequence things should go in
- What logically goes together
- What is ancillary, providing illustration, evidence or example to exemplify points made
- Whether the list is complete (you may think of things to add), or whether some things on it can be omitted *without* weakening the persuasive case. This latter point links to careful consideration of length (there is more about this later).

The quickest and easiest way to do this is to annotate your original note highlighting and amending it in a second colour. This is for your reference only; if you find it helpful to use arrows, circle words or draw symbols or pictures – fine, do so.

Stage 4: arrange the content

Sometimes, at the end of the previous stage you have a note you can follow and no more is necessary. Often however what you have in front of you is a bit of a mess. By arranging it I mean simply turning it into a neat list; this could also be the stage at which you type it out to finish the job on screen. Most people seem to input your own written material nowadays (I sometimes think the typing is harder work that the writing!).

Final revision is, of course, still possible at this stage but, that done (and it might include getting another opinion about it from a colleague) you are left with a clear list setting out content, sequence, and emphasis to whatever level of detail you find helpful. Some experimentation may be useful here; certainly I am not suggesting over-engineering the process. This sheet is the blueprint from which you write. You must decide the form in which such is most useful.

Stage 5: a final review

This may not always be necessary - or possible (deadlines may be looming) – but it can be useful to leave it a while – sleep on it – and only start writing after you come back to it fresh. You can get very close to things, and it helps you to see it clearly to step back from it and distract your mind with something else.

Now, with a final version of what is effectively your writing plan in front of you, you can – at last - actually draft the text.

Stage 6: writing

Now you write; or type or dictate. This is where the real work is, though it is very much easier with a clear plan for the task. What you have done here is obvious, but significant. You have separated the two tasks, one of deciding *what* to write, the other deciding *how* to put it. Being a bear of very little brain I for one certainly find this easier; so too do many other people. Some further tips:

- *Choose the right moment:* if possible pick a time when you are "in the mood". There seem to be times when words flow more easily than others. Also interruptions can disrupt the flow and make writing take much longer as you recap in your mind, get back into something and continue. It is not always possible, of course, but a bit of organisation to get as close as possible to the ideal is very worthwhile
- *Keep writing:* do not stop and agonise over small details. If you cannot think of the right word, a suitable heading – whatever – put in a row of xxxxxxs and continue; you can always return and fill in the gaps later, but if you lose the whole thread then writing becomes more difficult and takes longer to do. Again the idea of preserving the flow in this way can quickly become a habit, especially if you are convinced it helps.

So now you have a draft, though already you may feel that it needs further work. Now what?

Stage 7: editing

Few – if any – people write perfect text first time and alter nothing. If you write, then some editing goes with the territory. So, rule one is not to feel inadequate, but to accept that this is the way it works and allow a little time for revision. Careful preparation, as suggested in earlier stages, should minimise alterations; at least you should not be finding things you have left out, or needing to alter the whole structure. The words may need work however. Computer spelling and grammar checkers are very useful. Be warned however, not every spelling is corrected (for example, *their* and *there*); proper names and such like may need care too. Grammar checkers should not be followed slavishly, especially for the punchy style you need for some persuasive messages. Perhaps a sensible rule here is not to ignore anything highlighted as grammatically incorrect *unless* you can give yourself a good reason for so doing.

Editing may be helped by:

- *Sleeping on it* (as mentioned earlier)
- *Getting a colleague to check it* (maybe you can do a swap with someone else who would value your looking at some of their written material – it is amazing how a fresh eye and brain picks up things to which you are, or have become, blind. Incidentally, listen to what they say and consider it carefully, it is easy to become automatically defensive and reject what, with hindsight, may turn out to be good advice)

- *Be thorough* (do not regard editing as a chore; it is an inherent part of getting something right).

Editing is an important stage. Seemingly small changes: replacing a word, breaking a long sentence into two, adding more and better placed punctuation, all may make a real difference. This is the time to bear in mind style and use of language (see next chapter) as well as sense and clarity. Then, when you are happy with it let it go, - just press *print* or do whatever comes next. It is easy to tinker forever. You will always think of something else that could be put differently (better?) if you leave it and look again; productivity is important too.

Let your version of this systematic approach become a habit and you will find your writing improves, and that actually writing gets easier. As a rule of thumb, allow a proportion of the total time you allocate, or simply need, for writing to preparation. If you find that say 15–30 percent of the time, whatever works for you, is necessary, you will also find that rather than "additional" preparation increasing the overall task time, such jobs actually begin to take less time. Simply pitching in and starting immediately at the top of a blank sheet of paper (or computer screen) with no preparation is just *not* the quicker option that perhaps it sometimes seems to be.

If you are conscious of how you write and think about what makes the writing process easier or more difficult for you, then you will no doubt add to this list and adopt further ways that help you. Of course, at the same time we must be realistic. There are things that interfere with how you would like to write, including deadlines that prohibit putting it off and other priorities and interruptions. The right attitude here involves two things:

- Do not let perfection be the enemy of the good; in other words, get as close as you can to your ideal way of operating, do not let problems make you see the whole thing as impossible and abandon your good intentions entirely
- Use habit to build up greater writing strength; for instance persevering with something until you *make it work for you*. For example, I used to be rather poor at writing on the move, but a busy life and regular travel made it necessary. Nowadays, after some perseverance, I can switch out the hustle and bustle of, say, a busy airport and get a good deal done.

Summary

The message here is simple:

- Go about the task of writing systemically
- Create and work to a writing plan
- Separate deciding *what* you are going to include (content), from *how* you are going to put it (style)
- Fix on an approach that suits you and stick with it, creating individual habits in the process
- Give the task space and priority
- Check, check and cheque (sic) again.

5. LANGUAGE: THE PITFALLS AND OPPORTUNITIES

NEXT WE LOOK AT HOW use of language contributes to creating the right reaction and earning a reading. This is the first step to making language persuasive. To keep matters manageable, this topic overflows into the next chapter in which the specific way in which language can be made not just appropriate and acceptable, but actually persuasive is further investigated.

Here the key issues are to make what you write:

- Clear and descriptive
- Striking , even memorable
- Readable (above all)

And to avoid language that is:

- Confusing
- Incorrect
- Annoying

Looking around

As was said earlier communication is not the easiest thing to do well, and written communication – especially in organisational life – is one of the weakest methods. Prevailing practice leaves a little to be desired, especially in two respects:

- *Formula:* too much business writing seems to copy a textbook style, it is written as if following a prescribed pattern, albeit one that is old fashioned and which seems designed to persuade the reader that the writer could bore for their country
- *Gobbledegook and "business-speak":* if the style is archaic, the language is labyrinthine. It will be replete with sesquipedalians, places its full points overlong distances apart and allows an element of galimatias to act to confuse and obscure the sense – and another thing, it is without structure. Sorry, try again. It will be too full of long words, long sentences and has no recognisable structure to guide you through. Incidentally, sesquipedalian means a long word, takes one to know one I suppose. Galimatias is gibberish.

I exaggerate here; but not a lot, certainly bearing in mind some of the documents I have had to read over the years. So, if prevailing standards are somewhat low what does this mean? It is an opportunity; and a major one. Anyone who can create something that stands out as readable and more interestingly presented than most other things will earn a reading, and may score some points. So, the first intention to adopt here is one of following a different path. You are not trying to follow in the footsteps of some ancient order of business writers; rather you are trying to communicate with people in a way that they will like, pay attention to and compare favourably with anything else they read.

Think of some of the stock phrases you read in documents clearly written on mental "automatic pilot":

- *I would like to take the opportunity to*
- *...enclosed herewith for your perusal is ..*
- *Assuring you of our best attention at all times*

When you read such phrases your mind responds instinctively. You *know* the writer has been sitting in a dusty office for more years than they can count, and that they thought of you – the reader – not one single time as they switched the "standard reply" button on, and their mind off. If I exaggerate again (not much) it is to make a strong point that writing needs thinking about, and that when you do so what you are likely to write is going to be well removed from this sort of unthinking approach.

That said, let us consider what makes for writing that will have more impact and which is likely to allow you to make what you say persuasive. A number of points are considered in turn with some examples of each.

Understandable

This is where we began at the start of the book. So I will only summarise and add a few examples. The key things to watch out for are:

- *Using the right words:* is your proposal describing a *recommendation* or an *option?* Is your product *uncomplicated* or *easy to use?*

- *Using the right phrases:* particularly to ensure that they convey the full meaning you want: what exactly is *personal service* for instance? It presumably means more than that it is done by people, but the full nature of what the style of service is may need filling out
- *Wrong words and wrong arrangements:* some errors here are habits – the superfluous word *Basically* at the beginning of every (other) sentence may mean nothing but does not actually confuse. Starting a sentence with *At this stage...*on the other hand may imply a change later that you do not intend to imply. Similarly in mentioning figures you cannot say *about 10.7%;* it is either *about 10%* or precisely *10.7* (and all figures must be right, I am reminded of the football manager who said that 80% of his team would be in the next game; that is 8.8 people!). A wholly different impression of accuracy is given in these different ways. Another hazard is to find you are stating the obvious in an incorrect, or unintentionally amusing way: as does the old sign you still sometimes see in shops saying *Ears pierced while you wait* (or perhaps technology has moved on in some way of which I have yet to hear).

The next heading picks up a point that will act in numbers of ways to make things clear – and more readable.

Keep it simple

There can be exceptions of course, but by and large you should use:

- *Short words:* why write *presupposes* instead of *means*? Or *elucidate* when you can *explain*?
- *Short phrases:* do not write *attached herewith* when *attached is* says it all, and try not to use phrases that seem to come into common usage although there is a shorter, clearer alternative: so write *now* not *at this moment in time, to* rather than *in order to, if* rather than *should the situation arise that, because* rather than *due to the fact that* etc.
- *Short sentences:* writing overlong sentences is a common fault. Look at things you write and see if any long sentences can satisfactorily be divided in two. That said, a bit of variety is necessary, as nothing but short sentences can sound awkward and repetitive. Combinations of long and short help to produce a readable flow. Like this.

A favourite quotation helps me remember to favour simplicity. Mark Twain wrote: *I never write the word metropolis when I get paid the same for writing the word city.*

Length

In a busy life people always say they want something brief, but as was indicated earlier, the word just means short. This should not, in fact, be an end in itself, a better intention is to make things *succinct*, that is short but containing all the essentials to inform in an understandable way. Things that are not relevant should not artificially extend length, and you should remember that comprehensiveness is rarely (ever?) an option. If you wrote everything that you could about anything most of the content might be superfluous. This means selection is important, you need to decide what to write and what to omit (see comments about planning in Chapter 4). Writing style also affects length. A convoluted style will fill more pages, and there is an expression to the effect that you should *write tight*.

For example, look at the phrase below and see how many words you can abbreviate it to without changing the sense.

In spite of the fact that he was successful, it did not take him long before he was sorry that he had used so many words.

After thinking – note the comment about this below.

Writing tight

The phrase stated earlier that I suggested you attempted to abbreviate is 27 words long. The following, encapsulating much the same message consists of only 10.

Although he succeeded, he soon regretted using so many words.

I used this as an exercise on a course not so long ago and one inventive participant reduced it further – to 3 words: *Successful, but verbose* (and it very nearly does capture the full message of the 27 word original version!). Certainly this tightening is a good skill to develop.

Note: there is an important balance to be struck here. If you omit salient parts of a case, then persuasiveness may well be diluted – the argument is incomplete and lacks power. Make it too long and people switch off and do not read it all. The answer? If in doubt it is better to write more, provided you are sure that the extra points do, in fact, boost the case.

Style

You want it to sound as if *you* are writing and, as been said, to avoid a formulaic "business style". The best way to look at this is to think of what you would say, and then formalise it a little rather than seeing a need to put it into some separate sort of "written language". In addition, let us look at some specific dos and don'ts, first do **not** write in a way that is:

- *Bland:* this is a common failing, using words that have no precise meaning. Nothing you write about should be described as *quite nice* or *rather good*, what is an *attractive offer?* (if it is money saving, say so), what is, in a phrase beloved of the airlines, a *slight delay?* (an hour or endless hours?)
- *Patronising:* you should really know better than to be patronising or condescending; sorry again, suffice to say that you should be careful not to talk down to people
- *Biased:* your view may or may not be appropriate. Often it is not: is a manager likely to persuade a group of staff by saying *I think this is an excellent idea* ahead

of describing it, or would they do better by saying *Here is an idea to consider*?

- *Politically incorrect:* some things here have become the norm – *Chair* rather than *Chairman*, for example – but other things need some thought – and something like the he/she problem can make for awkward language. It is important to remember that although there are sillinesses in this area, it does matter and it is important not to upset people, for some of whom it may be more important than it is to you. The same can be said of the need to ensure that nothing written seems inappropriate to any minority group

- *Badly timed:* as language changes it is clear that words and phrases have a real life cycle. Use something early on and it can appear pretentious, use it too late and it can seem silly. Any example will date, so let us pick something that seems to me to be already past its best. The phrase *user friendly* was originally a neat description, now however that everything has been so described it has become essentially meaningless

- *Annoys:* the point here is that certain kinds of grammatical and linguistic error tend to be spotted and cause particular annoyance. Too little punctuation makes something awkward to read; and the current proliferation of wrongly used apostrophes annoys many people. Too few headings and space makes it *look* as if it will be difficult to read. Everyone has some pet hates. A widely held one concerns the word *unique*. This means "unlike anything else", nothing can be *very unique, a bit unique* or any *other* kind of unique for that matter. Anything like this (another is different *from*, not *different to*) is to be avoided

- *Introspective:* this is an important one for persuasive writing, and the main symptom is too much usage of words like I and we, and not enough of you. An example is often found in brochures: every paragraph, every sentence and every thought sometimes starts *We, The company, I* or similar and the net result is a catalogue effect that distances people from the content. Avoid!

Conversely, it is important that you **do** write in a way that is:

- *Respectful to the reader:* in the sense of reflecting their needs and to an extent being in "their language", certainly as has been said you can lose people by being too technical. Thus a memo to a group of staff of mixed technical experience needs to be carefully pitched and may need to say how it is dealing with matters
- *Precise:* say exactly what you mean
- *Positive:* have the courage of your convictions; there is rarely a place for *perhaps, maybe* and *I think* in persuasive writing
- *Descriptive:* this is an especially important one, people like it if something is well described, not just making it clear but painting a picture. Language is a powerful tool. The fact that even a very few words, provided

they are well chosen, can say so much more than the words themselves, illustrates this. For example:

- How much can just two words tell you about a person? Prolific author Isaac Asimov (who wrote more than 400 books, so I have a way to go yet!) is reputed to have been asked what he would do if told he had only six months to live; he replied in two words: *Type faster.* This surely says so much about the man, his writing, his attitude and more
- Even something as routine as a classified advertisement can make the point, for example: *For sale: baby's cot. Unused.* Have you ever read an ad that conjures up so much heartache?
- The following description (from Peter Mayle's book *A Year in Provence)* describes a visitor to the house, he arrives with an attractive young lady and shows her up the steps ahead of him. The only thing that is said about him is that he was - *A man who could give lessons in leering.* Is there anything else you need to know?
- It is also clear that any description can make something live if it is well, or memorably, phrased. There is surely all the difference in the world between something being *Somewhat slippery* and it being *As slippery as a well buttered ice rink.*

An allied point here is that where it is appropriate your *interest* and/or *enthusiasm* for something should show, and should often do so unequivicably.

Grammar and syntax

This book is not a guide to grammar, though such things clearly matter. Punctuation has been mentioned, and you may find a guide to some of the details of language use in this sense useful (more of this anon). Here, as an example of how incorrect things can change the nature of writing, particularly if a document is riddled with inaccuracies, I would mention just two examples:

- *Oxymoron:* care is needed here as an oxymoron (a two-word paradox) may sound silly – *pretty ugly* – or be used usefully – *deafening silence*. Or are open to debate – what about *trustworthy lawyer*?
- *Tautology:* this is unnecessary repetition and should be avoided. You should not write about *foreign travel overseas,* and there is no such thing as *future planning.* Planning must, by definition, be about the future; after all it would be difficult to plan the past. If tautology is *unnecessary* repetition, then perhaps we need a different word for inaccurate repetition. I say this having just seen a label on an electrical appliance reading: *Lifetime, 2 year guarantee.*

Finally, because more than a small amount of advice on grammar, syntax and form is beyond our brief here, a brief checklist of rules designed to stick in the mind ends this chapter.

Some *memorably put* writing rules

- Don't abbrev things inappropriately.
- Check to see if you any words out.
- Be careful to use adjectives and adverbs correct.
- About sentences fragments.
- Don't use no double negatives.
- Just between you and I, case is important.
- Join clauses good, like a conjunction should.
- Don't use commas, that aren't necessary.
- Its important to use apostrophe's right.
- It's better not to unnecessarily split infinitives.
- Only Proper Nouns should be capitalised. also a sentence should begin with a capital and end with a full stop
- Use hyphens in compound-words, not just in any two-word phrase.
- In letters reports and things like that we use commas to keep a string of items apart.
- Watch out for irregular verbs that have creeped into your language.
- Verbs has to agree with their subjects.
- A writer mustn't change your point of view.
- A preposition isn't a good thing to end a sentence with.
- Avoid clichés like the plague.

Summary

The most important things here are to:

- Use clarity as a foundation for your attempts to persuade
- Keep things simple (and brief, but without sacrificing the power of your message to persuade)
- Make language work for you, and avoid your style (or grammar, punctuation etc.) clouding the issue or actively annoying.

6. USING LANGUAGE TO BOOST PERSUASIVE POWER

NOW WE EXTEND THE THINKING of the last chapter and look at specific ways of making a persuasive case in writing. To begin with we will take a letter as the main example (with which memos and e-mail have things in common), though other kinds of document are mentioned later, many of the principles apply widely and there are some specific examples at the end of the chapter.

The letter
Whatever its role, and however it is delivered (it may be an email), this is a crucial document to get right and there are several factors to consider. First however we will consider the readers' reaction when faced with a letter to read

People seldom read a letter immediately, and rarely simply in the same sequence in which it was written. Their eyes flick from the sender's address to the ending, then to the greeting and perhaps the first sentence. They fix on headings, they skim to the end – and then, if the sender is lucky, back to the first sentence for a more careful reading of the whole letter from the beginning. So the first sentence is an important element in 'holding' the reader and it should arouse immediate interest.

This is something worth bearing in mind as you write and reinforces the point made earlier about *earning a reading.* In fact for some writing it may be worth calling a powerful image to mind. I always think of the training film *The Proposal* (Video Arts), which I sometimes use on courses. It starts with the sales person writing a proposal and imagining its receipt. We see the buyer (actor John Cleese) expressing overpowering delight at its arrival. He clears his desk, cancels meetings, and tells his secretary that he must not be disturbed as he settles down to read. Then the voice over says *But it's not like that is it?* The scene changes, and this time when the document arrives we see a surely John Cleese sitting miserably at his desk dropping Alka Selzers into a glass of water and wincing at the noise they make. Maybe *that* is more like what we should have in mind as we write!

When you do write, for some letters used in quantity, with customers for instance, an early decision concerns the salutation.

Dear who?

The salutation is an important item to consider. Numbers may preclude individual salutations. If you are not saying 'Dear Mr Smith', or 'Dear John', what do you say? One answer is nothing. Simply start with a heading (indeed an example shown later does just that). Doing so does not preclude you finishing with your name. Though in this case you should omit 'Yours sincerely' and set the name close enough to the text, so that it does not look as if the signature was forgotten. If numbers permit, always sign letters. Larger quantities can have the signature matched in, which still gives something of a personal touch. If you are only mailing small quantities you can actually sign each letter.

On other occasions a standardised opening may be necessary, for example:

Dear Client or Customer (that at least is clear)
Dear Sir
Dear Reader
Dear Colleague

Dear Finance Director (or other appropriate title) etc.

In many ways none of these are taken to be more than a token greeting and unless it is something really novel, will have comparatively little impact. If you can find a form of words you like, perhaps almost anything is better than 'Dear Sir/Madam'!

Giving it *persuasive* structure

In selling face to face, you can adapt your approach to the individual you are with as the conversation proceeds. In a letter this is not possible and a formula to structure the approach is useful. The classic sales acronym AIDA stands for:

Attention: first get them reading and wanting to know more

Interest: then develop their interest and make them want to read on to complete the picture

Desire: aim to turn just interest into an actual acceptance or wanting for something

Action: conclude by asking clearly for the action you want to be taken.

This provides a simple structure. It works well in providing a plan to help compose letters and represents accurately the job to be done in prompting a response. Each stage is worth a further word:

• **Attention – the opening**

The most important part of the letter is the start. It may well determine whether the rest of the letter is read. The opening may be quite short, a heading perhaps, a couple of sentences, two paragraphs, but it is disproportionately important. A good start will help as you write the letter, as well as making it more likely the recipient will read it. Omit or keep references short and make subject headings to the point – the reader's point. Do not use 'Re'. It is old fashioned and was used to show something was a heading before it was easy to do so with, say, **bold** type. Make sure the start of the letter will command attention, gain interest and lead easily into the main text. For example:

- Ask a 'Yes' question
- Explain why you are writing to that reader particularly
- Explain why the reader should read the letter
- Flatter the reader (carefully)

- Explain what might be lost if the reader ignores the message
- Give the reader some 'mind-bending' news (if you have any).

- ### *Interest/desire – the body of the letter*

The body of the letter runs straight on from the opening. It must consider the reader's needs or problems from their point of view. It must interest them. It must get them nodding in agreement: *Yes, I wish you could help me on that.*

Of course (you say) you are able to help them. In drafting you must write what you intend for the readers and then describe the benefits you can offer (not features), and in particular the benefits which will help them solve their problems or satisfy their needs.

You have to anticipate the reader's possible objectives to your proposition in order to select your strongest benefits and most convincing answers. If there is a need to counter objections, then you may need to make your letter longer and give proof, for example comment from a third party that the benefits are genuine. However, remember to keep the letter as short as possible, but still as long as necessary to complete the case. If that takes two, three or more pages, so be it.

It is easy to find yourself quoting the literature that may well accompany the letter to the reader. If you were writing a lecture on the subject, you would probably need all that information. When writing to a prospective customer you have to select just the key benefits which will be of particular value to the reader and which support the literature.

The body of the text must:

- Keep the reader's immediate interest;
- Develop that interest with the best benefit;
- Win the reader over with a second benefit and then further benefits.

- **Ending**

The next job is to ensure action from the reader by a firm close. This may need to summarise but beyond that the most important thing to do is to state, clearly, the action or agreement you want (we return to this in the next chapter).

An appropriate tone

Finally we return to the language you use: it must be clear, appropriate and have sufficient impact to persuade. The following points add to those made in the last chapter, starting with a checklist which recaps and sets out some basic rules for persuasive writing:

Be clear	Make sure that the message is straightforward and uncluttered by 'padding'. Use short words and phrases. Avoid jargon.
Be natural	Do not project yourself differently just because your message is in writing.

Be positive   In tone and emphasis (and be helpful).
Be courteous   Always.
Be efficient   Project the right image.
Be personal   Use 'I' – say what *you* will do.
Be appreciative   *Thank you* is a good phrase.

The next checklist, set out below, examines certain specific aspects of the language used in letters. All these examples are very much the kind of language that do *not* lend themselves to persuasion; while one or two such words or phrases may do no great harm, if this kind of style predominates that the tone set is wholly wrong. So:

Avoid trite openings
We respectfully suggest ...
We have pleasure in attaching ...
Referring to the attached ...
This letter is for the purposes of requesting ...

Avoid pomposity
We beg to advise ...
The position with regard to ...
It will be appreciated that ...
It is suggested that the reasons ...
The undersigned/writer ...
May we take this opportunity of ...
Allow me to say in this instance ...
Having regard to the fact that ...
We should point out that ...

Answering in the affirmative/negative ...
We are not in a position to ...
The opportunity is taken to mention ...
Dispatched under separate cover ...

Avoid coldness and bad psychology
I would advise/inform
Desire
Learn/note
Obtain
Regret
Trust

Avoid cliché endings
Thanking you in advance ...
Assuring you of our best attention
    at all times, we remain ...
Trusting we may be favoured with ...
Awaiting a favourable reply ...
Please do not hesitate to ...

Rather your text must be **positive**. It should say *this is the case*, *this will be what is done* and will rarely say things like *I think ...*, *Probably* or *Maybe*.

Experienced direct mailers talk about 'magic' words or at least words that inject a tone that should always be present, such can be consciously used in many documents. Some examples appear below (and you may be able to think of more).

Magic Words		
free	today	timely
guarantee	win	respected
new	easy	reliable
announcing	save	opportunity
you	at once	low cost
now	unique	fresh.

You must not overuse such words or your message will become blatantly over the top, but do not neglect them either.

You must keep searching for ways of making your text perform better. Again, the following is designed not only to float some examples, but also to show the approach you need to cultivate. The guidelines that follow are reviewed in terms of 'do's' and 'don'ts', with no apology for any occasional repetition.

The Don'ts
You should **not**:

- *Be too clever*   It is the argument that should win the reader round, not your flowery phrases, elegant quotations or clever approach.
- *Be too complicated*   The point about simplicity has been made. It applies equally to the overall argument.
- *Be pompous*   This means saying too much about you, your organisation and your product/services

(instead of what it means to the reader). It means writing in a way that is too far removed from the way you would speak. It means following too slavishly the exact grammar at the expense of an easy, flowing style.

- *Over claim*   While you should certainly have the courage of your convictions, too many superlatives can become self-defeating. Make one claim that seems doubtful and the whole argument will suffer.

- *Offer opinions*   Or at least not too many compared with the statement of facts, ideally substantiated facts.

- *Lead into points with negatives*   For example, do not say 'If this is not the case we will ...', rather 'You will find ... or ... '.

- *Assume your reader lacks knowledge*   Rather than saying, for example, 'You probably do not know that ...'. Better to say 'many people have not yet heard ...'. Or: 'Like others, you probably know ...'.

- *Overdo humour*   Never use humour unless you are very sure of it . An inward groan as they read does rather destroy the nodding agreement you are trying to build. A quotation or quip, particularly if it is relevant, is safer and even if the humour is not appreciated, the appropriateness may be noted.

- *Use up benefits early*   A persuasive letter must not run out of steam: it must end on a high note and still be talking in terms of benefits even towards and at the end.

The Do's

You should **do** the following:

- *Concentrate on facts* The case you put over must be credible and factual. A clear-cut 'these are all the facts you need to know' approach tends to pay particular dividends
- *Use captions* While pictures, illustrations, photographs and charts can often be regarded as speaking for themselves, they will have more impact if used with a caption. (This can be a good way of achieving acceptable repetition, with a mention in the text and in the caption.)
- *Use repetition* Key points can appear more than once, for example in a leaflet and an accompanying letter, even more than once within the letter itself. This applies, of course, especially to benefits repeated for emphasis.
- *Keep changing the language* You need to find numbers of ways of saying the same thing in brochures and letters and so on.
- *Say what is new* Assuming you have something new, novel – even unique – to say, make sure the reader knows it. Real differentiation can often be lost, so in the quantity of words make sure that the key points still stand out.
- *Address the recipient* You must do this accurately and precisely. You must know exactly to whom you are writing, what their needs, likes and dislikes are

and be ever conscious of tailoring the message. Going too far towards being all things to all people will dilute the effectiveness to any one recipient.

- *Keep them reading* Consider breaking sentences at the end of a page so that readers have to turn over to complete the sentence. (Yes, it does not look quite so neat, but it works.) Always make it clear that other pages follow, putting 'continued ...' or similar at the foot of the page.

- *Link paragraphs* This is another way to keep them reading. Use 'horse and cart' points to carry the argument along. For example, one paragraph starts 'One example of this is ...'; the next starts 'Now let's look at how that works ...'.

- *Be descriptive* Really descriptive. In words, a system may be better described as 'smooth as silk' than 'very straightforward to operate'. Remember, *you* know how good what you are describing is, the readers do not. You need to tell them and you must not assume they will catch your enthusiasm from a brief phrase.

- *Involve people* First your people. Do not say ' ... the head of our XYZ Division', say 'John Smith, the head of our XYZ Division'. And other people. Do not say ' ... It is a proven service ...', say ' ... more than 300 clients have found it valuable ...'.

- *Add credibility* For example, if you quote users, quote names (with their permission), if you quote figures, quote them specifically and mention people by name. Being specific adds to credibility, so do not say, 'This is described in our booklet on …', rather ' … this is described on page 16 of our booklet on …'.

- *Use repetition* Key points can appear more than once, in the leaflet and the letter, even more than once within the letter itself. This applies, of course, especially to benefits repeated for emphasis. You will notice this paragraph is repeated, either to show that the technique works or perhaps to demonstrate that some half-hearted attempts at humour are not altogether recommended!

"Devices": lessons from direct mail

The principles of writing persuasive copy for direct mail material are essentially similar to that for any other persuasive document, indeed to much of what has now been described. In addition, however, there are some tricks of the trade, as it were, that are used in direct mail that might prove useful in other kinds of communication. Here I want particularly to touch on what are called "*hooks*". What are hooks? They are a variety of elements that will generate the interest you want by focusing attention in a particular way. Here are some examples.

Combinations Featuring two things linked together in what is sometimes called the "strawberries and cream" method (in other words if you want to persuade someone to buy strawberries then not only do they sound more attractive coupled with cream, but you might just sell some cream too! This can be used in many ways, for example: a training department might try to persuade someone to attend a course and read a book first, the latter making the former more attractive – *as I know you are busy, reading this first will make even just a day's training useful*

Team
This is something to be responded to by more than one person. For example, a memo from a manager to the staff in their department might address, the team, different groups and even individual people on the way through, using the need for everyone to pull together to enhance the persuasive case to all concerned

Limited offer
Somehow things are more attractive if they are in short supply. Only a limited number can attend (a meeting, say); only limited stocks of a special product are available (or only until the end of the month)

Status
This involves describing something as an opportunity for people to be the *first* with something, such as meeting at a prestige venue or in doing or buying something new

A competition	Competitions and prizes are used extensively with product promotion. The prize may be the product itself (which costs the manufacturer or supplier less than it appears to be worth). It may be something simple like a bottle of Scotch, or more elaborate, like a holiday. Even internally this can be used, though then we probably call it an incentive – though it persuades none the less for that – *I must have this information in on time, so there will be a prize draw for all those people who meet the deadline*
Sponsorship	Link to an event, perhaps a charitable event, for example, "*Meet us on such and such a date and join us at the local theatre club where we are sponsoring the production of … in the evening*". Such might enhance many messages.
Flatter the recipient	You can refer to them in a way that makes them sound special, perhaps addressing them *As a member of the Board you will know that …*
Second chance	Write to people a second (or third) time as a 'reminder' designed specifically to increase the appeal (there is an example of this to come).

You can also highlight aspects of the overall message. Here are some examples.

Timing Describing an offer that will give people a benefit *before the holidays* or *by the end of the year*

Exclusivity An offer to a select group, for example, *only for clients*, *only for local business people*, or *only for men or women* (though carefully perhaps!)

Such factors as these are clearly not mutually exclusive. They can be linked, adapted and no doubt bettered. No one knows in advance what degree of gimmick will appeal, so be careful of course, but remember that the recipients will probably take a less censorious view than you of such matters. Some level of experiment may well prove worth while and if you are not prepared to be a pioneer, keep a sharp eye on what is done by others.

There is a good deal of detail here. Not every idea needs to be thrown into every document. In each case you have an armoury of techniques from which to select a range of things appropriate to the occasion.

Examples

Here we focus on a number of examples to illustrate some of the specific different circumstances in which persuasion is necessary. These are: an internal, department to department communication, a complaint, a press release, letters chasing debtors and finally, a simple direct mail letter (or rather two).

Internal selling

Here we need a short scenario to set us up with an example. Mr B runs the sales office for a medium-sized company. His team comprises of people who take customer enquiries, offer technical advice, handle queries of all kinds and take orders. Recent reorganisation has resulted in the merging of two departments. His people now occupy a large office together with another group, the order processing staff, (who deal with invoicing and documentation). For the most part, all is going smoothly. However, the routing of telephone calls has become chaotic. The switchboard, despite having a note explaining who handles customers in which area of the country, is putting two out of three calls through to the wrong person, and the resulting confusion is upsetting staff and customers alike as calls have to be transferred.

Mr B knows he must sort this out. He carefully drafts and sends a memo to the Personnel Manager, to whom the switchboard operators report, complaining that the inefficiency of their service is upsetting customers and putting the company at risk of losing orders. The memo sent is shown below:

Memorandum

To: Ms X, Personnel Manager

From: Mr B, Sales Office Manager

Subject: **Customer Service**

A recent analysis shows that, since the merging of the sales office and order processing departments, two out of three incoming calls are misrouted by the switchboard and have to be transferred.

This wastes time and, more important, is seen by customers as inefficient. As the whole intention of this department is to ensure prompt, efficient service to our customers, this is not only a frustration internally, it risks reducing customers' image of the organisation and, at worst, losing orders.

I would be grateful if you could have a word with the supervisor and operators on the switchboard to ensure that the situation is rectified before serious damage results.

He is surprised to find that far from the situation improving, all he gets is a defensive reply listing the total volume of calls with which the hard-pressed switchboard has to cope, and quoting other issues as of far more importance at present to the Personnel department. It concludes by suggesting he takes steps to ensure customers ask for the right person.

Mr B intended to take prompt action that would improve customer service, he felt he had stated his case clearly and logically, yet all he succeeded in doing was rubbing a colleague up the wrong way. The problem remained.

Think, for a moment, about how else this might be handled before reading on.

Here this initial communication was in writing. The memo Mr B emailed, though well-intentioned, had the wrong effect, and would also have made any kind of follow-up message (necessary because the problem had still to be resolved) more difficult.

The problem is certainly identified in the memo, the implications of it continuing are spelt out, and a solution - briefing of the relevant staff by the Personnel Manager - is suggested. The intention, as has been said, is good. However, despite a degree of politeness - "I would be grateful . . ." - the overall tone of the message is easy to read as a criticism. Further the solution is vague, tell them what exactly? It seems to be leaving a great deal to Personnel. Maybe he felt "it is not my fault, they should sort it out". To an extent this may be true, but you may find you often have to choose between a line which draws attention to such a fact or which sets out to get something done. They are often two different things, and the latter calls for a persuasive approach.

In this case the key objective is to change the action, and to do so quickly before customer relations are damaged. This is more important than having a dig at Personnel, and worth taking a moment over to get the message exactly right. It is, whilst a matter of overall company concern, something of more immediate concern to the sales office.

So what should Mr B have done? To ensure attention, collaboration and action, his memo needed to:

- Make the problem clear
- Avoid undue criticism, or turning the matter into an emotive issue
- Spell out a solution, or at least a suggestion
- Make that solution easy and acceptable to people in Personnel (including the switchboard operators themselves)

Perhaps with that in mind, his memo should have been more like the following:

Memorandum

To: Ms X, Personnel Manager

From: Mr B, Sales Office Manager

Subject: **Customer Service**

The recent merger of the sales office and order processing departments seems to have made some problems for the switchboard.

You will find that I have set out in this note something about what is happening and why, and specific suggestions to put it right. You will see the suggested action is mainly with myself, but I would like to be sure that you approve before proceeding.

The problem

Two out of every three incoming calls are misrouted and have to be transferred. This wastes time both in my department and on the switchboard, and is, of course, also likely to be seen as inefficient by customers. To preserve customer relations, and perhaps ultimately prevent orders being lost, the problem needs to be sorted out promptly.

The reason

Apart from the sheer volume of calls, always a problem at this time of the year, the problem is one of information. The switchboard operators have insufficient information to help guide them, and the departmental merger has outdated much of it. Given clear guidance neither they, nor customers, will have any problems.

Action

What I would suggest, therefore, are the following actions:

1. I have prepared a note (and map) showing which member of staff, deals with customers from which geographic area, and would like to make this available for reference on the switchboard.
2. This might be best introduced at a short briefing meeting. If we could assemble the operators for ten minutes before the board opens one morning, I could go through it with them and answer any questions.
3. Longer term, it would be useful if the operators visited our department and saw something of what goes on, we could arrange a rota and do this over a few lunch hours so that it can be fitted in conveniently and without loss of productivity.

If this seems a practical approach do let me know and I will put matters in hand.

This is not set out as the "right" or guaranteed approach, but it is certainly better. And it is more likely to work because it is designed specifically to be persuasive. Note especially that:

- It lays no blame
- It recognises that both Personnel, and the switchboard are important
- It considers their needs - for clear guidance, being able to handle the volume more easily, someone else taking the action
- It anticipates objections, Personnel wondering *who will do all this?* for instance and their not wanting any hassle
- It is specific in terms of action, who will do what and when (maybe it could have specified the timing more precisely).

There seems every chance it will have the desired effect. Many situations exhibit similar characteristics. All it needs is a clear, systematic approach that recognises the other person's point of view, and *sells* the desired solution and action.

Press releases

Notices sent to the press for promotional reasons are certainly specialist documents. They have duel persuasive objectives, first to persuade an editor to read them and write them up for publication, secondly to put things in such a way that any successfully resulting story is itself positive and persuasive. There is a need here to abide by the "rules", i.e. produce something that is in the form that editors and others want, and yet also make it stand out and get attention. The list that follows sets out the "rules" for press releases:

- It should carry the words "Press (or News) Release" at the top, together with the date (which should ideally go at the top left)
- If what is called an *embargo* is necessary (i.e. a request not to publish before a certain date, to ensure news appears as near as possible simultaneously in different publications) this should be clearly stated
- Start with a heading, probably not too long, but sufficient to indicate clearly the contents of the release and start to generate interest
- Space it out well, with wide margins and good gaps between paragraphs etc. This allows the recipient to make notes on it
- If two or more pages are used, make sure that the end of one page makes clear that there is more overpage (or break the sentence to prompt turning over)
- Similarly, when you are finished actually write "End" as the last word
- Use a "newspaper" style of writing that follows all the "keep it simple" rules of writing
- Watch the length, you need to make a powerful case, but be sure not to be unnecessarily lengthy or verbose
- The first sentence is crucial and must get people wanting to read on

- Avoid overt "plugging" (even if this is effectively what you are doing!)
- Try to stick to facts rather than opinions
- Opinions can be given in quotes and ascribed to an identified individual (this can work well and can link to a picture of the person concerned; and pictures can increase the chances of publication)
- Always label any separate attachments such as photographs
- Do not overdo the use of adjectives in a way that just seems exaggerated and jeopardises credibility
- Never underline anything for emphasis (this is used as a printing instruction meaning to put the words underlined in italic type)
- Separate notes to the publication from actual text, so that an instruction (like *photographers will be welcome*) cannot be mistaken for text and printed as part of the story
- Always include, at the end, clear details of who to contact for more information and exactly how to do so
- Make sure it is neat, accurate and well presented (and that it lists any enclosures)
- Do not cry wolf. Save releases for when you really do have something interesting to say, and do not send contrived ones that will simply act to put people off looking at any future ones
- Be enthusiastic about it. It is your story, so if you are not why should they be; enthusiasm is one of the few good things that is contagious.

The example that follows is not a million miles from home as it were but incorporates some of the principles set out in checklist form above.

Press Release

Date xxxx

Practical guidance on the gentle art of persuasive writing:
– a new book from Bookshaker.com

Business writing can be a chore. Finding the right words, ensuring clarity, and avoiding the classic business writing sins of writing gobbledegook or deteriorating into over formal "officespeak" can be a struggle. It is somehow more difficult than communicating face to face. When there is a particular objective like the need to make something persuasive, the difficulties compound. The new book Persuasive Writing offers practical advice to make this easier.

It reviews the whole process from the expectations of readers and setting clear objectives to a systematic way of getting down the right words and editing text into final form. The author, Patrick Forsyth, has a marketing background (he runs Touchstone Training & Consultancy) and the author of a number of other successful business books. He comments:

"Communication is never easy – who works for an organisation where there are never any breakdowns in communication? – and business writing, and persuasive writing in particular, is perhaps what many people find most difficult of all. This book, which reflects my experience with people on many business writing training courses, aims to present an accessible guide to the essentials of getting it right".

The book shows how to write clearly and effectively, how to make the message come over in an acceptable manner so that it persuades people to read, agree and take action. It is designed to increase the likelihood of success and reduce the time it takes to "put things on paper".

The book costs £8.99 and is published on 4th July 2014

Enclosed: - a photograph of the author
– a copy of the book's cover

For more information contact:
xxxxxxxxxxxxxxxxxxxxxxx (full contact details)

Complaints

Here the first job is to reduce someone's anger, resentment or annoyance – but also very often to persuade them of something for the future, for instance: accepting the offered solution and being willing to do business again despite the hiccup.

The two letters below need no lengthy commentary: the first is abrupt and unlikely to succeed in pouring oil on troubled waters or persuading. The second is a better approach.

Dear Mr Brown

Thank you for your letter of 20 January. You will see that you missed attending our seminar "Making Effective Presentations", which you were registered to attend on 18 January, because you misread the joining instructions. The enclosed copy shows that the correct details were certainly sent to you.

If you want to try again, the programme repeats on 18 March and will be conducted at the same venue. You will need to record your intention to attend in writing.

Yours sincerely

Dear Mr Brown

Your missing the seminar "Making Effective Presentations" on 18 January, when you were registered to attend, must have been very annoying. Indeed your letter of 20 January makes this wholly clear; and I am sorry to hear this.

In view of the short notice on which you planned to attend, while joining instructions sent to you did set out the correct details of date and venue (a copy is enclosed), we perhaps should have made it clearer. My apologies.

Luckily the schedule has this programme repeating before too long. I have therefore moved your registration forward to the next date – Wednesday 18 March – and I hope you will be able to put this in your diary now while places remain available. It will be held at the same venue. Full information about the course is again enclosed, as are details of the exact times and location involved.

Do let me know if this should not be convenient. Meantime, I am sure that you were able to put the unexpectedly available time on 18 January to good use, and that you will find the seminar useful when you are able to attend. We look forward to meeting you.

Yours sincerely

This is a simple enough situation, a misunderstanding on the part of Mr Brown rather than a more serious error that has to be sorted out and for which emends must be made. It is still an opportunity to impress the client, ensure the business is retained and set the scene to maintain any ongoing business relationship. It is this that the second letter addresses.

Chasing debtors

Most people hate chasing overdue accounts, but remember the old maxim, which says that: *it is not an order until the money is in the bank*. It is a job that must be done. There are some bizarre ploys like sending a postcard, thus displaying the debt publicly (at least to the postman), or writing "accidentally" to the wrong address so that again the matter is made public, perhaps in the office next door. More appropriate is a systematic approach that follows up and follows up again (but do not have a whole series of "final demands", people will quickly spot that you do not mean it – I once saw a series of eight letters *all* marked "Final demand"!).

Better is a fixed number of letters all of which assume the matter has been overlooked accidentally, but lay down firm action. Such a sequence might go as follows:

1. Dear

You may recall receiving our invoice (dated 27 November) about a month ago itemising the amount due for (details).

I am writing to you because this is overdue, perhaps it was simply overlooked, but I would appreciate payment promptly (adding details of how payment may be made). If there is any reason other than oversight why this has not been paid, please call (number) and ask to speak to Susan Jones who will be pleased to discuss the matter with you.

2. Dear

£1550-98: overdue since (date)

My accountant is now pressing me very hard to get this payment in. Very few customers seem to be as forgetful about payment as you appear to have been. Perhaps I may ask that a cheque be sent by return (again you may want to spell out alternative methods of payment, perhaps also restating the credit terms).

Prompt payment will save additional costs for us both, since I am now required to pass the matter over to a collection service if I do not hear from you, with your payment within 7 days.

If there is any problem you want to discuss, please telephone (number) and ask to speak to Susan Jones who will make every effort to sort it out.

3. Dear

£1550-98: collection arrangements

I have now written to you a number (you might specify) about this payment which dates back to (date) when our invoice clearly specified 30 day payment terms. As I have consistently received no reply, this matter is – as noted in my last letter – being passed over to a collection service. This will quickly involve you in legal costs.

I do hope that you are able to respond immediately and prevent this. Payment may be made by (list methods).

The intention here is to be reasonable, clear and invoke the letter of the law (people do after all know that whatever they have contracted for must be paid for). At the end of the day you must rule a line, write no more and put the matter on a legal footing. Note: once a threat has been made and does not materialise, most laggardly payers will infer they have even longer to bolster their own cash flow situation.

Incidentally, this is not a task that can be exclusively carried out in writing. Other means of communication may also be involved. One tip: if you also have to telephone, make the call not sitting at your desk, but standing up. It may sound silly, but it works because it helps you sound far more assertive; if you do not believe it, try it!

Direct mail

Direct mail in all its forms is a little beyond the scope of this book, though what is said here is relevant and may help if it is something you use. Many people, however, use simple sales letters of some sort that one might regard as on the fringes of direct mail. The following example is of a letter designed to be sent to people known to you (at least to some extent). In fact the two letters shown were designed together and it was planned to send them a few weeks apart. They worked well and the second one, sent to the same list (or rather to those on the list who had not responded to the first letter), produced very nearly as high a percentage response as the first.

They were sent with a simple factsheet and, except for a few close contacts, were not personalised in any way.

Tandem sales letters: letter 1.

**A one hundred percent
biased recommendation:**

Reflecting the special nature of the marketing of professional services (it is not at all like selling baked beans or ball bearings), my new book *Marketing & Selling Professional Services* is published this month by Kogan Page in association with the Institute of Directors. It offers practical guidance on how marketing applies to, and can be effectively implemented in, the world of professional services. One reviewer has already described it as:

"... an informative, accomplished and entertaining guide ... Copious in information, fundamental and practical in advice, this marketing handbook is a convincing and positive guide with a potentially long shelf-life" (*Practice Marketing* magazine).

As an absurdly generous gesture to those in the professions with whom I have crossed paths in some way, copies are available from here by returns and *post free*.

Details are enclosed. Orders sent here, together with the remittance, will be dealt with on this basis for the next month only.

So, complete and return the form – as they say in all the best promotions – *now*.

Best wishes .... PATRICK FORSYTH

Letter 2:

"We are making sufficient profit, thank you, and **don't want to make any more**"

You are almost certainly not, in fact, saying this but you did ignore my recent letter about my new book *Marketing & Selling Professional Services*. This was published just a couple of weeks ago by Kogan Page in association with the Institute of Directors. It offers practical guidance on how marketing applies to, and can be effectively implemented in, the world of professional services. One reviewer has already described it as:

"... an informative, accomplished and entertaining guide ... Copious in information, fundamental and practical in advice, this marketing handbook is a convincing and positive guide with a potentially long shelf-life" (*Practice Marketing* magazine).

You can receive a copy promptly and *post free* – details are again enclosed. Just complete and return the form with the appropriate remittance and, who knows, there may well be just a few ideas that can help improve your business profitability (if you want, of course). I hope to hear from you about this, and, of course, if I can assist in any other way do please let me know.

Best wishes ... PATRICK FORSYTH

These are well targeted, seemed to hit the right note and, at the time, offered something new and different – with the potential of it helping a business in a number of ways, not least financially. (The book is targeted at those people like accountants, lawyers and others who offer a professional service and work on fee basis; should you be in this sector you might like to note that it contains a chapter on using direct mail!). The small amount of graphic emphasis used here is, I think, about right to enhance the look and make the words work harder.

Summary

At this stage, although there is a good deal of detail to remember and use, the overall strategy is clear:

- The way a message is written needs care and consideration
- Small differences, literally a word or a phrase changed, can be significant
- The overall approach needs to reflect the readers perspective and specifically the way in which people weigh things up and make decisions
- The language needs to be used consciously to create understanding and impact
- The style should be accessible, not too far removed from how you would speak to someone, and any device that can add punch should be considered (though overall the net effect must not be too slick, artificial or gimmicky).

Now, because it is so important, we look at the final words of the message and the injunction to action that they should contain.

7. FROM PERSUADING TO PERSUADED

IN THIS CHAPTER WE LOOK at the final words used in persuasive writing and their relationship with intentions to prompt action. Then, after a word about presentation, we then go back to examining a complete message and look again at the letter quoted in Chapter 3.

Aiming to prompt action

As you close it may be useful to make a (short) summary of the benefits of the proposition. Having decided on the action you want the reader to take, you must make it *absolutely clear to them what it is*. Yes, and at the risk of repetition, the onus of communications is on the communicator, but ...enough. Suffice to say that reference to action must be clear, and perhaps that if any assumption is made it is that what needs to be done needs spelling out *very carefully*.

Reply cards with good direct mail are as well produced and important looking as the rest of the shot. They often reinforce or repeat their message more than once, for example, the telephone number to be called is printed bold, repeats more than once and is in colour. Similarly the instructions, carefully analysed, smack of belt and braces; it is perfectly sensible and worth learning from.

It is necessary to nudge your reader into action with a *decisive* close. Do *not* use phrases like these:

- *'We look forward to hearing ...'*
- *'I trust you have given ...'*
- *'... favour of your instructions'*
- *'... doing business with you'*
- *'I hope I can be of further assistance'*

Such phrases are only really added as padding between the last point and *Yours sincerely*. They are cliched and add nothing except an old fashioned feel or, worse, a feeling of uncertainty and circumspection. Instead, use real closing phrases.

Here are some examples.

The alternative close:

- Ask the reader to telephone or write
- To telephone or use the reply-paid envelope
- To ask for a meeting or more information.

Immediate gain:

- A phrase like: *Return the card today and your profitability could be improved* offers something extra, or seemingly extra, if action is taken now rather than later. The converse of this is called a *fear close* for example phrasing something to say *Unless you respond now* something good will be missed

'Best' solution:

- A phrase that summarises key issues mentioned earlier: *You want a system that can cope with occasional off-peak demands, that is easy to operate by semi-skilled staff and is presented in a form that will encourage line managers to use it. The best fit with all these requirements is our system 'X'. Return the card indicating the best time to install it* - that then links to a closing statement

Direct request:

Just a straight request, or even, on occasion, an instruction:

- *Post the card back today*
- *Telephone us without delay.*

An impersonal message can put people off taking action, so if it something like a letter going to a list of people make sure it is signed off appropriately. Consider, too, the person who should have their name at the bottom of the letter. Replies will tend to come back to them – and so will queries. So, for example for a sales letter should it be the sales office, one director or another and how well are they able to cope with any response? Make sure their name is typed as well, as signatures tend to be awkward to read, and that a note of the position they hold in the firm is included. People like to know with whom they are dealing.

PS: Remember the power of the postscript. Secretaries will tell you they are for things inadvertently left out, while direct mailers (and research about it) will tell you they really do get read. Make sure their wording makes clear they are not about something omitted, but are there to provide emphasis. Use them to reinforce an important point or to add a final benefit – it can add strength to the message.

PPS: Some people even use two! (but do not overdo this, it is the kind of thing that makes people compare your missives unflatteringly to *Readers Digest*; this despite their clear success).

One example here concerns a training centre I have worked at. Located in the depths of the countryside it is difficult to find and despite writing to delegates saying this, the map provided was often ignored and people turned up hot and bothered having got lost en route. A P.S. added to the letter used to provide joining instructions repeated the information in more strident form; and the number of lost people declined markedly.

A visual enhancement

Finally, remember that the end product should be neatly presented. This applies to every document – memo, proposal or letter. Basics first. It must look right. It must be attractively laid out, grammatically correct and well presented. In selling this is especially important since it gives the impression that it has originated in an efficient and reputable firm.

The letterhead itself is important to the image: an up to date yet not 'over the top' design is what should be aimed at and this is not easy. Additionally, remember that an email does not look like a letter, and can be deleted in a second; it is not always the best method just because it is easiest. Subjective judgements are involved. Ultimately, it is a matter of opinion and in smaller firms this can sometimes mean a safe compromise, which may dilute impact. Consider, too, whether your standard letterhead is right for direct mail purposes if this is used.

To ensure the finishing touches and add impact you should think about the following:

- Position the letter on the page according to the amount of the text. It is unattractive if there is a huge expanse of white below a very short letter. Position it lower down, in that case, or consider having two sizes of letterhead paper printed and put short letters on the smaller sheets.
- 'Block' paragraphs, with double spacing between each paragraph for greater clarity and smartness.
- Leave at least 1½ in at the foot of the page before going on the second page; leave a bigger space to avoid having only one or two lines (plus farewells) on the second page. A good deal of business material ends up annotated in some way, so more space actually makes this easier for people.

- Allow enough space for the signature, name and job title. It is better to carry the letter over on to another page, than cram it in at the bottom.
- Note, at the foot of the last page, the enclosures mentioned in the text and sent with the letter.
- Staple the pages together to avoid losses.
- Number the pages.
- Number the paragraphs when a lot of points have to be covered.
- Underline all headings or make them **bold**.

Remember: layout of this sort of material must reflect the style, the reader and the emphasis of the points being made. It can bolster a persuasive message by helping create emphasis and putting over a feeling of efficiency (in the way, for example, that listing enclosures can do).

Graphic emphasis can help keep people reading, guide them through longer texts and simply create a feeling of accessibility and care that itself promotes readability. Such emphasis can be made, in this age of the word processor, in a number of ways, with:

CAPITALS
<u>Underlining</u>
    Indenting
Bold type
~~**COLOUR**~~
Italics

While these features should not be overdone, they can be useful and, in whatever form and combination you select, should be well placed. As an example consider this book. It has (if the typesetter has done their job well) a modern look. Space is as important as what is there, and the overall effect is designed to make the text seem accessible both as you flick through on first picking up the book and also on reading. It is very different to the "textbook" style of old.

Summary

To ensure that what you want and are asking people to do has a good chance of being done, make sure it is:

- Clear
- Appropriate
- Convenient and easy (or as much as circumstances will allow)
- Confidently put, and perhaps even with a degree of assumption

8. GETTING IT WRITE (SIC)

In this final chapter we look at a number of examples to revisit and extend the points made to date. First, we return to the example of the letter from the conference hotel looked at earlier. The letter shown below restates the message in a different way:

Dear

Training seminar: a venue to make your meeting work well

Your training seminar would, I am sure, go well here. Let me explain why. From how you describe the event, you need a business-like atmosphere, no distractions, all the necessary equipment and everything the venue does to work like clockwork.

Our XXX room is amongst a number regularly successfully used for this kind of meeting. It is currently free on the days you mentioned: 3/4 June. As an example, one package that suits many organisers:

- morning tea/coffee with biscuits
- 3-course lunch with tea/coffee
- afternoon tea/coffee with biscuits
- pads, pencils and name cards for each participant
- room hire (including the use of a flip chart and slide projector)

---

at a cost of (sum) per head including service and tax.

Alternatively, I would be pleased to discuss other options; our main concern is to meet your specific needs and get every detail just right.

You will almost certainly want to see the room I am suggesting; I will plan to telephone to set up a convenient time for you to come in and have a look. Meantime, our meetings brochure is enclosed (you will see the XXX room on page 4). This, and the room plan with it, will enable you to begin to plan how your meeting can work here.

Thank you for thinking of us; I look forward to speaking with you again soon.

Yours sincerely

This is surely much more customer-orientated. It has a heading, it starts with a statement almost any meeting organiser would identify with (and with the word "your"). Its language is much more businesslike and yet closer to what someone would say. The latter is helped by expressions like: "... get every detail just right" (even leaving out the one word "just" would make it sound more formal); and "come in and have a look" in the penultimate paragraph, which is surely better than a phrase such as "to arrange an inspection visit".

The writer keeps the initiative and sets the scene for follow up action (while making that sound helpful to the customer and recognising that they are likely to want to inspect the hotel). Finally, it remains courteous, and putting the (one) thank you at the end makes it stand out and allows a much less formulaic first sentence and paragraph. Better I think, and a version that reflects many of the principles now reviewed.

Initiating contact

The letter example used relating to the hotel industry was a response. To ring the changes and provide another "before and after" example, here is a letter that is making the initial approach. The following is from a security company to the prospective new owner of a house (addressed to me just before I moved). People moving house do provide a good sales opportunity. People are often somewhat dilatory about security, but maybe the pleasure of a new house is likely to make thoughts of making it secure easier to sow.

The first letter is typical. Features orientated, containing too much unexplained jargon and formula officespeak, as a result, it sells itself short and makes an insufficient case out of what should be a strong one. It also has a real cliche ending and leaves the initiative with the recipient to come back to them, rather than retaining the initiative.

Dear Mr Forsyth

I understand that you have bought the house on Plot 28 at Saltcote Maltings.

As part of their service the developer has retained us as advisors on all aspects of security including:

- intruder alarm systems
- security lighting
- closed circuit television
- entryphones
- any special security problems you may have

I am writing to introduce my company and to offer our services in regard to security for your new home.

We are dedicated to promoting and performing to high standards and to demonstrate our commitment, we

- are members of British Security Industry Association
- have NACOSS (National Approval Council for Security Systems) certification
- adhere to BS4737 for equipment installation
- have ISO 9002 (quality management system) certification

Enclosed are illustrations of typical robust and unobtrusive equipment we use. An alarm system would normally comprise of a central control unit, keypad to set the system, PIRs (detection units), magnetic door contacts, alarm sounder and panic buttons.

You also have the option to enhance the protection and peace of mind provided by the system through connection to a central monitoring station. The monitoring station operates 24 hours a day, 365 days a year and can alert the police, a key-holder or anyone you specify. There are two options for connection to a central station - Red Care or Digital Communicator.

We can provide an annual maintenance and service contract which includes access to a 24 hour a day call-out service.

For further information please contact me on the above telephone number or complete and return the request form.

We assure you of prompt and diligent service.

Yours faithfully

The objective being set here is clearly to set up a meeting (on site). I think something along the following lines would have made me think better of them - and made a response more likely.

Dear Mr Forsyth

28 Saltcote Maltings - keeping your new home safe

You must be excited about your planned move. It is a wonderful location which, as formal security advisors to the developer, we are getting to know well.

Sadly any home may be vulnerable these days. And even a cursory glance at crime statistics gives pause for thought. No one wants the upset, loss, damage and feeling of fear a break-in produces; however, a little care can reduce risks dramatically.

What better time to check that security arrangements are satisfactory than as you move into a new home? You will want your house, possessions and family to be safe, and we can offer sound advice on just how prudent action can make that so.

It may well be that even minor additions to the standard house specification can improve security significantly, and add a feeling of well being. You can receive practical, expert advice - whether that is to fit just one more lock, or involves a full range of equipment: such as intruder alarms, security lights, entry phones or a full 24 hour monitoring service.

You will want to be sure any such advice is just that - sure.

We take our responsibilities, for both recommendation and installation, very seriously. Not only are we members of the British Security Industry Association, we also have NACOSS (National Approval Council for Security) certification and adhere to other quality standards.

Sound advice

Some of the equipment we use is described in the enclosed brochures. But our first concern is to meet your individual requirements, and recommend what suits you best.

You can arrange for a visit and discuss matters in principle without any commitment; we will never over engineer the solution, and will only offer practical recommendations (not least to match your insurers requirements). You can contact me at once and arrange a meeting, otherwise I will call you soon to see how we may be able to help.

Good security follows sound advice - and saying: *it will never happen to us*, is really just not one of the options.

Yours sincerely

P.S. Talk to us in good time - installation done as a new house is completed can ensure wiring is hidden and avoid mess after you move in.

Both these letters were sent – indeed they were designed to be sent – with brochures. It is impossible to illustrate a whole brochure here, but a few comments are pertinent.

Brochures and leaflets

These may be items used in a number of ways: for example, brochures salespeople distribute, leaflets you display in a reception area or items used from the sales office or for direct mail. Similar principles apply to copy on web sites. There is, however, no reason why such material should be suitable for everything and you may need to produce dedicated material, tailored specifically to one specific task. Here we focus primarily on brochures sent by post whether en mass or one at a time.

In either case, the brochure is unlikely always to set out to tell people "everything there is to know" about the organisation, product or whatever, rather it may prompt a desire for discussion. Too much information can even have the effect of reducing responses. One hotel, sending direct mail to prompt its conference business, found that the numbers of potential clients coming to inspect the hotel doubled when they replaced a short letter and glossy comprehensive brochure with a longer letter, no brochure and an invitation (because people seeing the full brochure felt no need to visit, they could *see* what the place was like).

The production of brochures generally is an area of increasing professionalism and great care is needed in defining the objective, creating the right message and making sure the brochure looks good and reflects the image which the firm intends to project. The days of the bland, general brochure, very similar to those of other industry competitors, which describe the chronological history of the firm and everything it does and intended to be used for everything, are rapidly passing. What is needed now is the ability to match each objective in every particular area with something specifically designed for the job. This may mean producing separate brochures for each product. It may mean that any "corporate" brochure is a folder with separate inserts aimed at different target groups or different types of customer. It may mean a revised brochure every year. It may even mean a difference between the sort of brochure that is right to give a prospective customer after a preliminary meeting and the sort that is suitable to present to an intermediary who may have a role in, say, recommending you to others. It is "horses for courses".

For mailing purposes the brochure or leaflet concerned must be specific to the objective set for the particular promotion. Brochures may need to be reasonably self-standing, after all they may get separated from the covering letter (the two together almost always produce a better response). However, the total content – letter plus brochure – needs to hang together, to produce a complete and integrated message.

Overall, what must be created is something that is accurately directed at a specific group, with a clear objective in mind and – above all – that is persuasive.

This may seem basic; of course, promotional material is there to inform, but it must do so persuasively. That is the prime purpose. But this does not mean moving to something that is inappropriately strident (which might in any case be self-defeating), and it does mean putting a clear emphasis on customer need and benefits (what things do for people, rather than what they are).

Essentially, a customer focused approach (not anything introspective), and well designed for its purpose, is the rule. What does this mean? It must:

- Look good (though good design is much more readily available than good text)
- Be practical (for example for mailing and filing if you hope people will keep it)
- Be illustrated (almost always this enhances appearance)
- Be readable, interesting and relevant with its message being put across in a punchy, perhaps novel, way

There are a few rules to be observed about brochures and those rules that one might define are made to be broken. This is because they must be *creatively* constructed to reflect the image of the firm graphically, differentiate it from its competitors and aim their chosen message directly at the target group addressed. But the copy is perhaps more important than anything. Many brochures have clearly had a good deal of money spent on their design and print, but the text is dull or inappropriate.

Start with the copy – taking on board all the principles set out here – and then design the brochure as a vehicle to carry your message.

Social media

When the famous scientist Stephen Hawking published his book "A Brief History of Time" he was told that sales would halve for every mathematical equation he included. He settled on just one and the book sold millions. I don't delude myself that this volume will sell in the same sort of quantity, but social media are surely a current factor of the same sort – without mention of them this book would lose credibility … and perhaps sales.

So let's start with a tweet:

Social media are an important current communication method, but have one major factor that makes their effective use difficult. And that's a

Wait a minute, tweets are limited to a maximum of 140 characters. I was going to write: *Social media are an important current communication method, but have one major factor that makes their effective use difficult. And that's a strict limit on the number of words you can use.*

This enforced brevity makes for problems, one common to most such media, and certainly it makes the chances of ambiguity much more likely as people abbreviate to an extent where the precise meaning they seek to impart is diluted or even lost. The problem is compounded by the apparently natural tendency that so many people have to pay less attention to – and take less care over – brief messages such as they send on all electronic media. For instance, do you know an organisation, department or person who has not instigated a misunderstanding by unthinkingly dashing off an email? Be honest. What's more such misunderstandings can quickly turn nasty and do real damage.

Yet social media of all sorts can play a valuable part in sales and promotion. Many organisations have a Facebook page, many use Twitter, and other such sites and various other devices from LinkedIn to YouTube. Blogs are also used quite widely with promotional intent. All such things can certainly be useful; if there is a problem here (one beyond my brief here) it is that undertaking all such activity is time consuming. You need to consider very carefully on which you will spend time, then monitor how useful they prove and fine-tune your usage in light of results.

So, having decided what to spend time on, that is what suits you, what writing approaches help make your use of such special media effective? Two things are worth mentioning here (with the reminder that most things mentioned earlier also apply here):

1. *Select a manageable focus*: this is perhaps best described by an example. I have a book published called *Empty when half full* (Rethink Press). This is a critique of communication with customers and the public that has gone wrong (an example is the sign saying *It is dangerous to cross this bridge when this*

notice is underwater). I want people to buy it and thus want people to know various things about it, including that it is:

- Hilarious
- Ideal as a gift
- Useful: it's a sobering lesson in how difficult it can be to write a single sentence and get it right
- Well reviewed: in other words it is not just the author saying it is good
- Good value: and both myself and Amazon will send it post free
- Written by an author who has other titles published: again an evidence statement
- Hilarious: did I mention that?

So, clearly some choice - focus – is necessary here if you plan to write a 200 word blog or whatever, more so, if you only have 140 characters to play with. An essential strategy here may be to take things in small bites, focusing on one (or two) factors then more with another communication, and another, so that your total message builds up over time.

2. *Write tight:* this was dealt with on page earlier, including an exercise. You need to develop the habit of making your message both clear and succinct. This means taking a moment to précis text that is too long (against a background of having first selected an appropriate focus – you don't want to mention

everything and end up making nothing clear). This is made easier with practice; for example, I have written a huge number of articles over the years, always to a specific brief: 300 words, 1500 words or whatever. These days I am very accurate, I can usually get very close to the target word count with my first draft. So, useful habits build with experience and you can encourage this by being aware of the necessity.

Certainly the main lesson here is that the nature of what you are writing for, from a letter to an email to a blog or tweet, influences how text must be written. There is an old saying that makes a good point here: *given oranges, the job is to make marmalade*. Given 500 words (or any other specific length), the job is to select a content and style that will fit; creating a piece that reads well and does the job you want despite the restriction on length. Enough said: this section had to be 8/900 words and is now 854 – so I'll stop.

Follow up

Now we address a problem that many (most?) people find difficult. Letters that are the second or third in a sequence (or more, persistence is part of the sales process!) *are* perhaps psychologically difficult. You fear rejection, after several follow up attempts have been ignored you *know* that the recipient is avoiding you and, in any case, you may also feel that your best shot has been sent. So thinking what to write next is not easy. Such letters can:

- Repeat key issues (but must find a different way to say at least some of their message)
- Simply remind (with strong contacts this may be all that is necessary)
- Offer different action (the first says "Buy it", the second says "let us show you a sample").
- Aim to find some more novel way of continuing the dialogue.

The following example is of the last of these; a novel approach. It makes the point that sometimes there really is little new left to say, just "it's me again", especially if the proposition is good and the only reason for lack of confirmation is timing or distraction rather than that the customer is totally unconvinced. In which case, the job is to continue to maintain contact, and ultimately to jog them into action, while appearing distinctive or memorable in the process.

Following writing a short book for a(nother!) specialist publisher, I was keen to undertake another topic for them in the same format. I proposed the idea and got a generally good reaction; but no confirmation. I wrote and telephoned a number of times. Weeks turned to months – result, nothing. Always a delay or a put off (you may know the feeling!). Finally, when a reminder of the possibility came up yet again from my follow up system, I felt I had exhausted all the conventional possibilities, so I sat down and wrote the following:

> **Struggling author**: patient, reliable (non-smoker), seeks commission on business topics. Novel formats preferred, but anything considered within reason. Ideally 100 or so pages, on a topic like sales excellence sounds good; maybe with some illustrations. Delivery of the right quantity of material - on time - guaranteed. Contact me at the above address/telephone number or meet on neutral ground, carrying a copy of *Publishing News* and wearing a carnation.

I must confess I hesitated a little over whether to send it (it was to go to someone I had only met once), but at the end of the day I signed and posted it. Gratifyingly it did the trick and the confirmation came on the following day (and you can read the result - *The Sales Excellence Pocketbook*: Management Pocketbooks).

Sometimes a slightly less conventional approach works well. You should not reject anything other than the conventional approach; try a little experiment and see what it can do for you.

It helps you write if you read. The more interest you take in language, then the more it will influence you. There is no harm in copying examples of style and approach that appeal to you or in adapting and tweaking things for your own purpose. As well as reading, and observing more consciously, books or indeed anything else, keep an eye out for things that might particularly help. For example, if you must write sales letters keep a file of those that come to you (you might file them in two categories: those with good things in them and those that demonstrate what to avoid!).

Last, a recommendation: always have by you a good dictionary, a thesaurus (something for which there appears to be only one word! And which is a dictionary of synonyms) and a good guide to grammar. Something like the *Good Word Guide* (Bloomsbury) is useful, but I would also recommend a book by the novelist and columnist Keith Waterhouse – *English our English* (Penguin). This is the only grammar book you might actually enjoy reading. It is full of good advice, of enthusiasm for language and in places it is amusing. It will tell you when to use a colon rather than a semi-colon, but it will also encourage you to break a few rules and make your writing more interesting. I have read and reread it; and could usefully do so again.

Ultimately what constitutes the best persuasive writing is not something that follows a slavish set of rules; rather it is what does actually persuade. So do note, and record, your successes and failures and use what you have done to assist you in future. Some ideas or approaches may become part of your style. Others may be used again and doing so even once may be useful. Similarly, analysis will have you resolving never to do some things again. Experimentation is a useful part of the process, but so is learning from experience. Some of the ideas presented in the previous pages may well help you, but remember what the American essayist Clarence Day said: *Information's pretty thin stuff, unless mixed with experience*. At the end of the day what will make your written messages persuasive - is you.

FURTHER READING

THIS BOOK HAS MAJORED ON short messages, primarily letters and emails. If you want to revisit the area of business writing then let me make a completely biased recommendation, see:

How to write Reports and Proposals, Patrick Forsyth, Kogan Page.

This has a focus on longer documents, which for some people present their own problems, but which are just as important to get right.

SOME FURTHER BOOKS BY PATRICK FORSYTH

THE FOLLOWING ARE ALL PRACTICAL, **designed to encapsulate proven approaches and techniques and kick start effective action in these areas – all "career" skills, that is vital to both the individual and the organisation.**

How to write Reports and Proposals: **a revised edition published in association with the** Sunday Times **newspaper**

How to Motivate People: also published in association with the *Sunday Times*

Developing your Staff: (also with *Sunday Times)* a manager's guide to all aspects of gaining improved results from training and development in all its forms.

Successful Time Management - also in the *Sunday Times* series; a new edition continues to make this my bestselling title

Management Pocketbooks I have five books in this series of "mini-texts" on **negotiation, selling, starting in management, managing upwards (managing your boss)** and **managing meetings**

Getting a top job in Marketing: published in association with *The Times* – a guide to those wanting to get into and on in marketing

Getting a top job in Sales and Business Development also in the series above

Smart things to know about Becoming a Consultant – setting up, winning and doing the work - part of the *Smart* series

Manage your boss – this sets out how to create a positive and constructive relationship between managed and manager.

How to craft a successful business presentation and effective public speech – a new, up to date look at an important topic

Surviving office politics – a humorous look at the workplace with some common sense about how to deal with office politics along the way.

Winning business in the property sector – a book on personal sales technique aimed at the special world of architects, surveyors etc.

100 Great Sales Ideas – a book of 100 individual double-page spreads all highlighting ways to maximise the effectiveness of sales techniques: I have written two other books in this series, **100 Great Time Management Ideas**, and **100 Great Presentations Ideas**

The gentle art of getting your own way – selling – persuasive technique – for non-sales staff and the layman

Improve your coaching and training skills – another title in the *Sunday Times* series (directed at managers rather than trainers).

Difficult decisions solved in 90 minutes – an antidote to avoiding putting off or fudging those things that are awkward, difficult or embarrassing.

The PowerPoint Detox – a guide to enlivening presentations and using slides in a way that enhances what you do and avoids "death by PowerPoint".

Marketing: a guide to the fundamentals – published by *The Economist* this is a definitive guide for the non-specialist and a detailed overview that demystifies this vital, and oft misunderstood, function

Negotiation skills for Rookies – a review of negotiation in this special format

A recent book looks at techniques for surviving hostile economic times – **Tough tactic for tough times.**

Disaster Proof your Career – a review of tactics to conduct your career in a way that takes you forward and makes you less likely to be overlooked or eased out of an organisation.

Persuasion – a guide to communications that must be persuasive

Meetings – an agenda for success – a practical guide to what can too easily be an unconstructive timewaster.

Managing Change – the latest *Sunday Times* title: surely a must for anyone wanting to keep up in these dynamic times.

ORDERS: check with the author – via www. patrickforsyth.com – for prices, publishers and ordering process. All these books should be widely available via booksellers including web sellers such as Amazon and an increasing number are now available to download.